INSIDE THE MIND OF
TED BUNDY

Also available

Inside the Mind of Jeffrey Dahmer, Christopher Berry-Dee
Inside the Mind of John Wayne Gacy, Brad Hunter
Inside the Mind of the Yorkshire Ripper, Chris Clark and Tim Hicks
Inside the Mind of Rose West, Tanya Farber and Jeremy Daniel

INSIDE THE MIND OF
TED BUNDY

TANYA FARBER AND JEREMY DANIEL

G:

Published in 2025
by Gemini Gift Books
Part of Gemini Books Group

Based in Woodbridge and London

Marine House, Tide Mill Way
Woodbridge, Suffolk IP12 1AP
United Kingdom

www.geminbooks.com

Text and Design © 2025 Gemini Gift Books Ltd

ISBN 978-1-80247-271-4

Printed in the UK
10 9 8 7 6 5 4 3 2 1

Prologue

On a cool and mild morning in late January 1989, a doctor in Raiford, Florida, lifted his hand to write a few brief notes in the execution log at the state prison not far from where a man sat lifeless in an electric chair with a hood over his head.

Name of prisoner: Theodore Robert Bundy.
Date of death: 24 January 1989.
Time of death: 7.16am.

And with that, one of America's most chilling reigns of terror at the hands of a single and secretive man had ended.

But, more than three decades later, the twisted mind of Ted Bundy is still an endless source of fascination to members of the public. Part disgust, part intrigue, this attention to the workings of his mind is hardly surprising: his actions were so abominable and so outside of what the average person considers normal that it stands to reason he would still be gazed upon as a complete oddity.

We would do well to note as a society, however, that Bundy's despicable crimes did not occur in a vacuum. The lives he destroyed do not deserve less attention than his. The potential of the young women he killed and the brutality with which he treated them give insight into how lacking in empathy he truly was and how he viewed his victims as nothing more than prey.

The young lives he cut short were not simply statistics in a story with a serial killer in the main role. They had lives and ambitions, friends and family who loved them, rich identities that should define them as so much more than just "Ted Bundy's victims".

The cat-and-mouse story of his being brought to book also stands as a grim reminder of what happens when the authorities fail to reconcile their stereotype of a killer with a well-spoken college student who oozes charm and charisma.

And just as importantly, the story of Ted Bundy is a clear illustration of how far law enforcement still had to go back in the 1970s before the advent of digitized records, officials communicating outside of their silos and across states, and the potential for the criminal justice system to move with the times as new forms of forensic evidence and record keeping come to bear on catching criminals.

This book is thus an exploration of the mind of Ted Bundy within the context in which he was living. It explores his childhood and upbringing, his romantic relationships with various women and his uncanny ability to simultaneously live a "normal" life for some hours of the day while carrying out his heartless butchery during other hours of the same day. It considers the type of sickness of the mind that would, for example, lead a man to fake an injury and thus prey on the most sympathetic of women whose paths he crossed.

It delves into the efforts of law enforcement, as well as the glaring gaps in their work, and follows the public's experience of this unfolding horror story across time and states far flung across the vast American landscape.

It also, for the reasons given above, goes beyond the moment of murder in the lives of his victims and those who survived his brutal attacks. They all had more to offer the world, with healthy minds that might have taken them in a variety of directions where they could have lived extremely rich lives and made amazing contributions to society.

But ultimately, this book tells the story of how countless lives were shattered when one deviant and defective human being set himself up as a hunter within the social context of normal human beings whose minds are bent towards kindness, community and avoiding cruelty to others.

Ted Bundy was the exact opposite. He was driven by one thing only: his burning desire to harm young women.

1

In the Beginning

On a late autumn day in 1946, Eleanor Cowell, a young woman of 22, climbed into the back of a car belonging to the local minister and looked back nervously at her two sisters watching from the upstairs window of their large suburban home. The minister's wife turned on the ignition and pulled away slowly. The young passenger watched her parents standing on the sidewalk as the car moved off. Her father, unsmiling and stern; her mother, looking nervously up and down the street to see if any of the neighbours saw Eleanor leaving. Her baby sister Julia waved, and Eleanor raised a hand to say goodbye, then turned resolutely to face the journey ahead.

Eleanor, known to everyone she grew up with as Louise, settled in for a long journey. The journey from the suburb of Roxborough in northwest Philadelphia, the capital city of the state of Pennsylvania on the east coast of America, to Burlington, Vermont, was over 500 miles long and would take more than 12 hours to complete.

She passed by the sprawling factories that had sprung up during the Second World War as part of the manufacturing boom that had lifted the United States out of depression. She had come of age as the war stole many of the young men she had gone to school with, but it had also set the stage for a boom in manufacturing that would make the United States the envy of European nations scarred by years of war. The ceasefire a year earlier, on 2 September 1945, had ushered in a new era of hope for stability, prosperity and the traditional values of American family life. But Louise would not enjoy the same hard-won prosperity and the promise of a brighter future that so many of the other young women of her generation would who were starting their families in the post-war boom.

A few months earlier it would have been a very different story. Louise was the president of the young people's group at her church. She was looked up to by her peers. But after her pregnancy was discovered at a conference, she faced immediate ostracization and was pressured to leave the group. So it was that Louise found herself in radically different circumstances: single and unmarried with a belly swelling from the presence of a child. This was the furthest thing from good news for her and her family, and it changed everything. Now her destiny would not be defined by a baby shower in one of the many Victorian houses with proud mothers, aunties and friends festooning her in balloons and passing her one gift after another. There would be no gift packages of diapers, bottles and baby clothes from the friends she had grown up with. There would only be secrets. Louise was being whisked away to the confines of a secluded home hundreds of miles away where no one would find out about the "shameful" act of falling pregnant out of wedlock. Fate was taking Louise to a place where her every move would be scrutinized and dictated by the nuns in whose care she now found herself.

But in truth, her life before this scandal of unmarried motherhood had been far from the idyllic American dream. She had grown up in a large, religious household. Her mother, also called Eleanor, was withdrawn and depressed, while her father, Samuel Knecht Cowell, in particular, was a foreboding character who was described as a "tyrannical bully" and was thought to treat both human beings and animals in an abusive manner.

There were reports from neighbours and family members of Samuel swinging cats by their tails and kicking the family dog. It also later came to light that he had thrown one of his daughters – either Louise or her younger sister Audrey – down a flight of stairs merely for oversleeping.

His wife, by contrast, and probably in response to Samuel's temperament, was timid and obedient. Throughout her life, she had struggled with severe mental illness and mood swings. She was sometimes held in the grips of a dark depression that had her unable to leave the house or communicate with others, yet at other times she had manic episodes during which she would talk excessively and find it hard to calm down.

With hindsight and today's more sophisticated psychiatric diagnostics, these symptoms suggest she likely suffered from bipolar disorder long before she met Samuel. But when she found herself living under the same roof as a violent and unpredictable man, her mental health only deteriorated further.

She eventually became so depressed living in this household full of fear that she was given several courses of electroconvulsive therapy, a popular treatment for the more extreme psychiatric disorders at the time.

And so, with this family life as the backdrop, it is difficult to imagine what the younger Eleanor might have been thinking or feeling as she made her way to an unknown future in Burlington, Vermont, with her baby in utero.

It is likely she felt shamed and belittled, and that her pregnancy had become such a source of embarrassment to her religious parents that they offered little by way of emotional support. Neither did the minister's wife, who took her all the way to the Liz Lund Home for Unwed Mothers, then dropped her off and headed back home again.

As Louise gathered her few possessions and walked past the flower beds and between the tall trees leading up to the front door, a whole new era in her life had begun.

Louise was shown to the room where she would be staying until her "illegitimate" child was born, and she saw many of the other young women who found themselves in a similar predicament to her. It soon became abundantly clear that the next few weeks of her pregnancy would be spent in the presence of other such young women from around the United States, each of whom had had the misfortune of falling pregnant outside of wedlock, as well as a group of nuns who were not shy to express their disapproval and dish out harsh treatment.

On paper, the home was intended to provide refuge for unwed mothers, but in reality, the atmosphere was often strict and uncaring. Many of the young women behind the building's tall facades would have quickly experienced the judgemental attitudes of the nuns and the dehumanizing act of sometimes being called by a number rather than a name. Nevertheless, there were opportunities to bond with other young women in the same predicament, but Louise failed to do so. She was characterized as being "aloof" and many of the girls said that Louise "felt that she was above them".

The Liz Lund Home for Unwed Mothers was typical of the era.

By the time Louise Cowell found herself walking through the doors of her new temporary home in 1945, there were approximately 400 such homes across the United States, catering to a fast-growing number of women who society was set to reject through no fault of their own.

Each year, an estimated 20,000 to 25,000 women were admitted to such maternity homes in the United States during this period. Many of these women, labelled "fallen" or "ruined", faced isolation and were often required to use false names to protect their identities and had very limited contact with family and friends. They were also required to perform chores as part of their stay.

The societal stigma of an unwanted pregnancy was felt just as keenly inside the big Victorian homestead in Burlington, Vermont, as it was out in public life. The home was intended to hide "shameful" mothers away from the public gaze, and the nuns could be harsh and unsympathetic towards the inhabitants.

Like every other unwed mother of the era, Louise's fate was shaped by falling outside of societal norms and expectations. For example, when she went downtown, she was told to pick a wedding ring from a bowl near the home's front door so that people wouldn't stare at a pregnant woman without a ring on her finger. She, and every other woman there, was checked in under the surname "Lund" in order to hide their real identities.

These were methods of societal control in reaction to what was perceived as deviant behaviour. Doctors and psychiatrists diagnosed out-of-wedlock birth as tangible evidence of social deviance and pathology. Psychiatrists pointed to "illegitimate" births as a sign of the mother's psychological neurosis, and researchers at Harvard University even characterized unwed mothers as "psychiatric problems" and as "victims of … severe emotional and mental disturbance".

Nevertheless, and despite all the imposed prejudices against her, the pregnancy progressed as nature intended, and on 24 November 1946, on a cold wintry day, Louise gave birth to a son, Theodore Robert Cowell who weighed in at a perfectly healthy seven pounds and nine ounces. There were no complications during birth, but there were many complications to come.

For Louise, just 22 and with no family around her, the profound experience of giving birth "in secret" behind the closed doors of the maternity home was deeply confusing. On the one hand, like so many other women in the same circumstances, the expectation was that she would give up her newborn son for adoption and return to her normal life. On the other hand, she felt the tug of maternity straight away and did not want to be separated from her son.

A significant percentage of women – around 80 per cent – who stayed in such maternity homes were expected to surrender their children for adoption before they had a chance to bond with them. This trend was driven by societal pressures and a lack of support for single mothers in an era that would become known as the "baby scoop era". The prevailing belief at the time was that these women would be much better off separating from their newborns to maintain family honour and societal respectability rather than living as single mothers. As such, they faced coercion and pressure from family, social workers, doctors and clergy, who often presented adoption as the only viable option. The stigma surrounding unwed motherhood was so intense that many new mothers felt they had no choice but to yield to pressure and give up their babies for adoption. After relinquishing their children, adoption professionals instructed them to return to their lives as though the children had never existed, often assuring them that no one would ever discover their secret. As a result, many mothers kept silent about their surrendered children, never mentioning them again and perhaps wondering in silence for decades to come how their lives had ended up.

For Louise, just as for the many other women in the home, contact with her newborn baby boy, whom she had named Theodore (or Ted for short), was severely curtailed. Breastfeeding and changing nappies were the only moments she could share with the boy who lay in a small metal cot alongside scores of other babies who were also identified by number rather than name. The focus of such institutions was on facilitating adoptions, and as a result, maternal bonding was not encouraged.

As for the father of the baby, the story was – and still remains – murky. Louise told a story about the father that many found unconvincing. She was working as a clerk at an insurance company in 1946 when she met a man "through a friend at work". She claimed to not remember the name of the friend, and as for the man, that he seduced her and then abandoned her within a few weeks, leaving her pregnant and alone. Another theory in the neighbourhood was that Louise had been seduced by an older, married member of the church congregation who had swept the young woman off her feet during a church weekend retreat.

Ted's birth certificate listed his father as "unknown", but several theories have emerged over the years. One is that his father was an air-force veteran named Lloyd Marshall, with whom Louise had that brief romance. Another name sometimes cited is that of a sailor named Jack Worthington, but not only is there no proof he fathered Ted, there is also no proof of his actual existence.

The most disturbing theory of all, but one that also lacks definitive evidence, is that Louise's own father, the abusive man who ruled the house with an iron fist, was in fact Ted's father too. In that theory, Samuel raped his own daughter and impregnated her, which would make him both Ted's grandfather and his father as well.

The theory also sheds a disturbing light on the twist in the story that was to follow: not long after giving birth, Louise packed up her bags, shed the Lund name, left the maternity home behind her and tried to resume the life she had known in Roxborough. Not much is known about her state of mind, other than that she said at the time that she would remain in Philadelphia only if she was accepted; otherwise, she would go someplace far away. Not much is known about how she spent those first months after returning to the oppressive household of her strict father and the scene of her shame, or how her son Theodore fared as a newborn in the care of strangers while waiting for adoption.

But one way or another, after two months of separation during the cold winter of 1946, Louise's family decided that it was better for a family member to grow up with the family. Apparently at the end of the day, it was Samuel who decided that he wanted the baby to grow up under his roof after all, provided that nobody knew that he was the child of Samuel's eldest daughter. And so it was that in the early months of 1947, the same car that had arrived at the door of the Liz Lund Home pulled up once more, this time not to drop off the "ruined" unwed mother but to pick up her needy offspring and drive almost four hundred miles south back to Philadelphia.

This time, when she stepped back through the doors of the family home carrying the small bundle in her arms, Louise Cowell would prepare for her role in the "damage control" that her family had concocted for the small, innocent baby: from henceforth, anyone who asked would be told that he was the adopted child of Eleanor senior as his mother and Samuel as his father. That meant that young Ted would grow up thinking that Louise, his mother, was only a big sister.

2

Childhood

From the moment Theodore (Ted) Cowell arrived wrapped in a blanket at the family home in Roxborough, Philadelphia, his early life would be shaped by the web of deceit spun by his large, complex family. The woman who held him in her arms and posed as his mother was, in fact, his grandmother. And Louise, the young woman who suffered the isolation of giving birth alone in a home for unwed mothers with no love or support from her family members, was forced to bite her tongue, curb her maternal instincts and live her life as the baby's big sister.

But this falsified family configuration was only one of the problems that the family faced. The Cowell household was just as tense and violent as it had been before Louise had left, only now there was an extra person in the house, an impressionable little boy whose early childhood was marked by the goings-on in the house. His aunt Audrey felt certain that the "father issue" never being resolved for Ted was certainly a factor that contributed to the troubles that plagued him through his life.

Samuel Cowell, Ted's grandfather (and remember, possibly his biological father too), created a very negative blueprint for how a man should behave. He was often aggressive and intimidating to others, but he seemed to have a genuine soft spot for the young boy, and like all small boys, Ted adored his "father". Time and again, Samuel illustrated to the young Ted how easy it could be to wield power by creating fear in others. Ted was of course too little to understand this in the same way an adult would, but it certainly would have made an impression on him.

A revealing portrait of Ted in a 1989 issue of *Vanity Fair* magazine reveals that "Grandfather Cowell was 'an extremely violent and frightening individual' ... A talented landscape gardener, Cowell was obsessed with the delicate alpine plants that he nurtured. He would kick dogs until they howled and swing cats by the tail if the animals got near them. According to Louise's youngest sister, Julia, he would 'get so mad that he would jump up and down' and rage at the men who worked for him."

Samuel Cowell was the oldest of seven siblings, and even his own brothers were afraid of his violent outbursts. Although his primary tool of abuse was verbal, Louise revealed many years later that Samuel did on occasion beat his depressed and withdrawn wife, Eleanor. Ted's young mind didn't take long to cotton on to the fact that generating fear in others also afforded one a great level of power and influence.

Increasingly, scientific research is proving how important these early formative years are on the development of a person's brain and how neural pathways develop according to what a child experiences in the first few years of life. When infants and young children are raised in a violent household, they have very few other social references for what's normal as they have limited social interactions outside the home.

"Children exposed to violent discipline systematically show lower levels of socio-emotional development and are more likely to show violent behaviour towards other children and adults," according to Unicef.

It is, however, important to note that although violence in the home during early childhood is a major risk factor for problematic behaviour, it is by no means a definitive cause. Bluntly put, a great many children the world over are exposed to violence in their early years and do not become serial killers like Ted Bundy.

Violence and intimidation were not the only factors at play in the Cowell house. That same *Vanity Fair* article reveals: "According to one of Ted's cousins, Cowell, a deacon of the church, hid pornography, which the boys pored over as toddlers, in the greenhouse. Other relatives say he was a bigot who hated blacks, Italians, and Catholics." None of this seemed to register negatively with a young Ted. Despite witnessing these troubling traits in his early years, Bundy would later go on to describe his grandfather in the fondest of terms. He would later claim that he admired him and could identify with him as the only strong male figure in his life.

The marked contrast with his grandmother, Eleanor, must have shaped his understanding of men and women. Although she was framed as his mother and acted as his primary caregiver, her struggle with severe depression and repeated trips to hospitals for shock treatments made her rather unavailable to her son. This only compounded the dysfunctionality of the household. In short, family life negatively influenced Bundy's psychological development and shaped the complex personality that would later manifest itself in murderous behaviour.

And what of his relationship with his real mother, Louise? Over the years, the conventional wisdom was that Ted Bundy had a perfectly normal childhood. But a revealing death row interview with Doctor Dorothy Otnow Lewis, a highly respected 51-year-old New York psychiatrist, told a different story. The white picket fence, *Leave It to Beaver* childhood story that mother and son both told about their lives was something that drew deep suspicion from Dr Lewis. The *Vanity Fair* exposé that was based primarily on Dr Lewis's findings states, "Louise herself maintains to this day that she didn't suffer from a sense of shame within the family or outside: 'I had no problems whatsoever with anyone.' However, there is evidence that she was made to feel deep shame and had ample motivation to abhor this unborn, unwanted child." Like her father, she rarely discussed her true feelings and preferred to put a brave face on everything.

But even decades before he plunged Seattle into fear during his first bout of killings, in fact even when he was only a toddler, the signs would indicate that a violent path possibly lay ahead: his aunt Julia, whom he believed to be his sister, was fast asleep in bed one morning when she woke up to the image of a ring of sharp kitchen knives that had been placed around her. Next to the collection of weapons stood a small boy with a mischievous smile and a look of anticipation on his face, as if he was intrigued to see how his "sister" might react. This event is often referenced as an example of Bundy's early signs of disturbed behaviour, though it's difficult to assess how much weight it carries in foreshadowing who he would become. Dr Lewis was quite clear in her assessment of that incident, saying that such "extraordinarily bizarre behavior" in a toddler is seen, "to the best of my knowledge, only in very seriously traumatized children who have either themselves been the victims of extraordinary abuse or who have witnessed extreme violence among family members."

It might only be with hindsight that this incident is such a clear indication of what was to unfold.

It was at the age of five that Ted and his mother finally left the family home in Philadelphia and headed north for Washington

State. This was allegedly at the insistence of various family members who were aware of how violent the household was and how Samuel's tyranny shaped the atmosphere on a daily basis.

Louise, with her pretty face, crescent-shaped brows above eyes that seemed in a permanent smile and wavy brown hair in a bob with bangs, made the 3,000-mile journey to the northeast of the country – far enough away from her problematic parents to feel relieved that she was now beyond her father's grasp.

For young Ted too, raised by this same man, there may have been some liberation in no longer living under the dark cloud of the head of the household's bad moods and violent temper. On the other hand, there was always an understanding that the relationship between Ted and his grandfather was strong and caring. "You do have to wonder about the separation from the grandfather," said Dr Lewis. "Ted went away with a very angry, rejecting, cold woman who didn't really want him, who took him away from the one person who was really warm to him."

Louise had proclaimed that she would settle in Philadelphia provided that her community did not stigmatize her for what had happened. The fact that she packed up all her worldly belongings and drove all the way across the country seems to indicate that forgiveness for the crime of being an unwed mother was not exactly forthcoming.

She travelled almost as far as she could go, to the city of Tacoma, just south of Seattle, with her son Ted to start a new life.

It was here, as Ted grew into a young man, that more and more signs would emerge of Ted's sinister and strange nature for those who were watching closely. But they all played out against a backdrop of normal boyhood experiences and nothing outwardly obvious that Ted was anything other than a little American boy with short straight blond hair and an innocent face.

At first, Ted and Louise moved in with Louise's cousins Alan and Jane Scott. Some believe this sudden and short-lived insertion into a more affluent lifestyle shaped his aspirations and, later, feelings of inadequacy. His cousins had an air of sophistication about them. Trips to Europe and a comfortable life were taken for granted in their household, and this made an impression on the young Ted.

A year after the move from Philadelphia to Tacoma, Louise met a man named Johnny Culpepper Bundy. He was a hospital cook, and the two had first met at a singles night. Before long, Ted found himself living in a humble clapboard home on Sheridan Street, Tacoma, or as he described it later in the tape recordings made behind the bars of a prison cell, "the second house from the corner on the west side of the street".

Louise and Johnny went on to have three children, and Ted adopted his stepfather's surname of Bundy. Thus began a phase in his childhood that he would describe nonchalantly as "not being an unpleasant one".

Like so many other children living in American suburbs that border pockets of natural landscapes, his childhood was a series of fun and adventurous days that played out close to the family homestead.

He and all the other children in a four-block radius would ride their bicycles up and down the streets that criss-crossed between the houses. They would kick a ball in the field and, as Ted himself described of quality time spent with friend Warren Dodge, "We would fish off the pier across from the railroad tracks."

He said, "I remember those days of roaming with my friends. I remember the adventure and exploration of it all."

He spoke about this phase of his childhood in tones of reverence: playing marbles with the neighbourhood gang, hunting in the woods and thinking of himself as a "frog hunting champion" in first grade and boasting about his ability to "see those bulging eyes bob just above the surface of a murky pond".

On paper, it was your all-American childhood: long summer days spent outdoors and snowmen and warm little coats in winter. When a journalist visited Ted's mom to speak about his childhood, she produced an array of mementos: "His elementary-school report cards: a blizzard of 'A's and 'B's, with a few notes about helping Ted to control his temper and to 'develop a respectful, cooperative attitude toward the other pupils.' Birthday cards from Grandmother Cowell: 'Just think, you are four years old. Quite a big boy!' Christmas pictures: a much larger Ted towering over his four half-brothers and half-sisters. The girls wear crinolines and corsages and fold their hands in their laps – miniatures of their mother in the exact same pose. The boys wear bow ties."

Deliberately curated or not, there seems to be no hint that his caregivers had any idea that he was not your typical boy thinking typical thoughts.

Neighbourhood friend Sandi Holt tells a different tale. Since the horrors of Ted's serial killings were laid bare, she described the contrast between the ordinariness of both Ted and his family, and the subtle yet sinister clues of his status as an outsider to society.

Sandi's older brother was the same age as Ted – two years older than Sandi herself – and as such, she spent substantial tracks of time with him in his boyhood as they played in the suburbs.

She also got to know the family very well.

Sandi said the family could not have been more "Beaver Cleaver" if they tried. She was referring to a fictional television show from the '50s entitled *Leave It to Beaver*, the family of which became synonymous with your typical wholesome family with perfect children who are well-balanced and clean living.

In Tacoma, there was a clear distinction between the haves and the have-nots, and the Bundy clan fell distinctly into the latter group, but even so, their lives were enriched with all the routines and traditions of a wholesome American family.

Sandi recalls the facts of this: Louise worked as a secretary. Johnny was a "good dad". They attended church on Sundays and were very active in the Cub Scouts and Brownies movements. The kids went to church camps, and the parents were very involved in their lives.

But Sandi's close-up experience of Ted as a young boy also afforded her the opportunity to see him as a misfit despite everyone's best efforts to have him blend into the happy suburban scenario.

Other sources have augmented this notion – that Louise and Johnny did their utmost to include him in all family activities, yet he struggled to bond with his siblings and stepfather.

"He was just different," Sandi would later tell documentary makers. "He had a big problem with a horrible speech impediment and he got teased about it a lot. He just didn't fit in, even at boy scout camp, he just couldn't get the hang of tying the knots or shooting the gun or winning the races."

She said that even back then, he had a temper and "liked to scare people".

And that is where one sees the early roots of his sadistic behaviour.

Sandi recalls how Ted would dig a hole, or a "tiger trap" as she calls it, in the forest or woods and then place a sharpened stick upright in the middle. He would then cover it with loose vegetation to disguise it and watch to see what victim would get caught out by this childhood boobytrap.

She remembers how one little girl was running along and fell straight into the tiger trap, with the stick ripping a long and deep wound all down the side of her leg.

According to Sandi, by the time he got to high school, the feelings of inadequacy disguised by boastfulness were magnified.

"In high school, he wanted to be something he wasn't," she says. He wanted to be president and "show the world" that he was the one to reckon with. But this way of being, she was convinced, was all "blowhard talk".

His own descriptions on the recorded tapes bear out Sandi's notion that he spoke himself up to cover what was lacking.

He says of himself in his high-school years, "I did well in academics. I ran for office. Most of my close friends played football. We were on the track team and went skiing. I was one of the boys."

In sharp contrast, Sandi says, "He tried to fool you and would lie to you. He wasn't athletic. He wanted to be number one in class but he just wasn't. He just didn't seem to be all there, all present. There was a gap in him."

As for his sexual awakening, from the very beginning it seems to have been different and extreme. Ted told a therapist that he was such a compulsive masturbator as a teen that he even used to relieve himself in closets at school, leading to some humiliating encounters with gangs of boys who found him in the act and doused him in ice water, all the while cackling with humiliating laughter.

There are other records of him telling small lies and exaggerated stories, showing that his propensity for manipulative behaviour began at quite a young age.

There was one nocturnal activity that clearly had a huge influence on Ted's development and seemed to point the way to what he would become. As a teenager, he became a very committed Peeping Tom. He used to sneak out of the family home at night and walk around the neighbourhood, peering into bedrooms and trying to see women undressed or in their most private moments. He also started digging through garbage cans and dump sites looking for old pornography and detective magazines that featured pictures of women being tied up and victimized. When he found them, he would tear out the pages and keep them as trophies that he would return to again and again.

When Ted had a casual job at a department store, he simply took what he wanted and items that he knew his parents could not afford – he wanted ski equipment and stuff for his room, so he just took it and told his mother that they were "gifts" from the job because they appreciated him so much. He was also caught stealing a car towards the end of his high school career, which would have had grave repercussions on his college career if he had been prosecuted. But the famous Bundy luck held and Ted was let off with just a warning.

Yet, despite all of this troubling and anti-social activity, the picture he and his mother painted of himself over and over again was of a normal but introverted teenager.

He described himself as "not going to the dances or beer drinking", but he added, "I was straight but not a social outcast." His mother insisted, "From the time he was born Ted had as much love as anybody."

Sandi says he was good-looking but didn't date anyone and nobody got close to him. He was shy and introverted.

"I didn't dislike women," he said, "and nor was I afraid of them. I just didn't have an inkling what to do about them."

These utterances, in light of what he went on to do, are chilling.

But the most disturbing of all is his own assessment of himself as someone who didn't seem likely to follow the path he did.

In the *Conversations with a Killer* documentary, Bundy says, "Everyone is fascinated with the notion that there is cause and effect, that we can put a finger on it and say, 'Yes his father beat him when he was a boy, we could see it when he was a kid'. But, there's nothing in my background that would lead one to believe I was capable of committing murder."

3

The Up-and-coming Republican

Ted Bundy completed his high school education in 1965 with a sense of relief and a readiness to embrace the destiny he saw for himself. In his mind, he had only been wasting time in high school, and he was more than ready for big changes to occur. Since he was a young boy, Bundy had believed that he was destined for better things, and he knew for a fact that his route to the upper echelons of society ran through a prestigious college. Yet his belief in himself was never quite matched by his results. At school, Ted had spoken of himself as if he were part of the academic elite, but his grades were never more than average. He was smart, but he was no genius. These delusions of grandeur extended onto the sports field as well – he fancied himself as a serious athlete, somehow believing that he actually was one, when in fact he was barely ever picked for any of the teams that represented the school. The only sport where he was reasonably proficient was skiing.

So when it came time to apply to colleges, in the cold, harsh light of graduation, armed with run-of-the-mill SAT scores, he simply did not have the academic record that he so desperately desired. As a consequence, Bundy enrolled at the University of Puget Sound (UPS) in 1965 for his freshman year.

There were several practical reasons that made UPS a good choice for him. Firstly, it was a reputable college even though it was not part of the elite Ivy League. Secondly, it was right on his doorstep in his hometown of Tacoma, which meant he could continue to live affordably in his childhood home. And thirdly, staying where he had grown up meant he could carry on with the secretive nocturnal activities of spying on the neighbourhood women that had become such a central part of his identity.

When he enrolled at college, Bundy had no clear career path in mind and very little sense of what he wanted to do or what he was passionate about. It was almost as if he valued the idea of college more than college itself. He simply craved success, and he was infatuated with the idea that college would open doors to a better life far more than he liked the idea of hard work and deep contemplation. In that respect, he was no different to many other freshmen starting out in the world. His lack of a plan didn't exactly mean he would stand out as an anomaly. But already, his perception of who he was was at odds with the reality. A local, liberal arts college with a broad palate of options suited his needs at the time.

The beautiful 97-hectare campus of the University of Puget Sound had long been a nurturing environment for young people taking their first steps out into the world. When Bundy arrived in 1965, the era of flower power was in full bloom. All around him, young men and women were throwing off the shackles of conformity and finding their individual voices. The Beatles and the Rolling Stones were at the top of the charts, Bob Dylan had gone electric, war was raging in Vietnam, the Civil Rights Act had been passed by the United States Congress and the intoxicating feeling of change was rooted in the nation's colleges. However, the era of free love and the idea of overthrowing the establishment didn't resonate with Ted Bundy at all.

His political views were solidly Republican and a far cry from the pervading zeitgeist of the 1960s. He described himself as "somewhat of a conservative. I just wasn't too fond of criminal conduct and using anti-war movements as a haven for delinquents who like to feel that they are immune from the law. I did speak out about these radical socialist types who were just all for trashing buildings and destroying the university."

In the liberal northwest of the US at that time, Bundy's orthodox views made him stand out among his peers, and he felt marginalized and unwelcome by those who were perceived as being "cool".

His early foray into higher education was nothing short of disastrous. By the end of the first year, he dropped out of the University of Puget Sound and transferred to the University of Washington (UW) in the neighbouring city of Seattle with a plan to study Chinese. In this regard, he was ahead of the wave. It would be another six years before an American president would take the unprecedented step of visiting China. But Bundy had rightly surmised that, after decades of being misunderstood and isolated, China was on the cusp of emerging as a major player in international affairs and a global power to be reckoned with. Showing a remarkable sense of foresight, he reasoned that a fluency in Mandarin would be a valuable asset to have in the workplace, and that it would set him up for a career in diplomacy or international relations.

The idea was excellent in theory and would have stood him in good stead, but once again when it came to the classroom and doing the work, all his plans seemed to falter. Learning to speak a new language and interpret the Chinese characters known as Hanzi proved to be way too arduous for Ted Bundy. It's unclear how much of the language he actually learned in his first two years at college, but it was likely very little. Once again, his ideas about himself and what he was capable of achieving were at odds with his lived reality.

Nevertheless, some aspects of his life were going well, even if academically he was still floundering. Socially, he had come a long way and learned to project an appealing image on campus. He had toned down the establishment rhetoric in order to fit in better with his peers. Reflecting back on those years in conversation with journalist Stephen Michaud, he remembered that "at university, I was a nice, presentable, affable person. I compensated a lot for what I consider to be my most vulnerable aspect, my introversion, by being seemingly aloof, arrogant and intellectual but nice and tolerant and that kind of stuff."

After being somewhat of an outcast at UPS, Bundy was learning to become something of an expert at the art of fitting in at UW. His lack of academic progress and even his nascent political ambitions were mere background noise and an afterthought to the arena where his true passion lay – which was with a young college student named Diane Edwards.

It was the spring of 1967 when Ted Bundy fell properly in love for the first time in his life. Even though her name was Diane, Ted used the initial "S" when he wrote about her in his diaries. She was a beautiful, poised young socialite, 21 years old, from the wealthy enclave of Burlingame, California. In her high school yearbook photo, Diane stares confidently at the camera, looking graceful, relaxed and utterly in charge of her destiny. Her intelligent eyes, strong features and dark hair parted down the middle gave her an air of casual elegance. Her high school yearbook reveals she was the kind of person who volunteered at Red Cross, played volleyball, worked on the Christmas pageant and was awarded Posture Honours for the way she carried herself. Her whole life, she had grown up in a privileged, loving family, and it had given her the confidence to effortlessly navigate college and the world around her in a way that Bundy could only dream about.

The two of them had first met outside his dorm room at the University of Washington. Initially, Ted admired her from afar but didn't approach as he believed she was way out of his league. Diane was a little older than him; she was further along in her college career and came from a well-to-do family, giving her status and power over a teenage freshman. At first, he believed that he had no chance with Diane for all of those reasons, and because everyone said she was only into football jocks. But Bundy was nothing if not lucky, and it wasn't long before he caught a break in the form of a long car ride with Diane to take a skiing trip into the mountains north of Seattle. In the car, he used the opportunity to turn on the charm, which he followed up with a genuine display of one thing that he could genuinely do well – ski. More than that, he already had an innate ability to figure out what people wanted to hear and then give it to them. It all went according to plan, and the trip culminated in Ted managing to pique Diane's interest in him and secure a second date, then a third and a fourth. In no time at all, Ted Bundy was involved in a love affair that would go on to shape his personality and affect the rest of his life.

Bundy's biographer Ann Rule, who worked alongside him at the Suicide Hotline and wrote the book *The Stranger Beside Me* about Bundy, believes that Diane was the woman that Ted Bundy lost his virginity to. In her, "he saw a woman who was the epitome of his dreams", Rule wrote. "[Edwards] was like no girl he had ever seen before, and he considered her the most sophisticated, the most beautiful creature possible."

"She inspired me to look inside myself and become something more," he said, when reflecting on those heady early days with Diane.

Over the next few blissful months in 1966, they went out together on dinner dates, took frequent skiing trips and made love in his dorm room or in the back of her car out in some secluded nature spot. Ted was overly impressed with her car. He couldn't stop talking about it. There was nothing he liked more than to take a trip out into the countryside with a beautiful, sophisticated woman by his side. This, finally, was everything that Ted Bundy had ever wanted. "She's a beautiful dresser, beautiful girl," he said. "Very personable. Nice car, great parents," he said. "So you know, for the first-time girlfriend, really that was not too bad." With Diane on his arm, he felt accepted into the social strata that he had aspired to for his whole life.

Those descriptions of Diane read as strangely superficial and betrayed how his craving for social status outweighed his need for genuine love and affection. It was almost as if there was an inability to see her as a real, well-rounded and flawed person. All he saw was what was visible on the surface.

Academically, Bundy was still going nowhere fast. Eventually, he faced up to the fact that he was never going to get a degree in Chinese, so in 1968, he switched courses again, dropping Chinese studies and signing up for classes in urban planning and sociology. But once again, neither of those disciplines appeared to capture his imagination, and it wasn't long before he dropped out of college altogether and started working a series of low-paying jobs, such as delivery driver and retail store clerk, that were, frankly, an embarrassment to Diane and her socialite friends. But his political aspirations were moving in the opposite direction to his dwindling academic prospects, and he latched onto them as the new path forward – the same year that he dropped out, he also began volunteering in the Seattle office of Republican presidential hopeful, Nelson Rockefeller. Known by his nickname "Rocky", Nelson Rockefeller was part of the enormously wealthy Rockefeller dynasty and had served in the administrations of Presidents Roosevelt, Truman and Eisenhower. He made three attempts during the 1960s to become the Republican presidential nominee, including in the year 1968 when Bundy was working for his campaign, but he never successfully won the nomination to lead his party.

One of the highlights of 1968 for Ted Bundy was the opportunity he was given to travel to Miami, Florida, as part of the Washington state delegation to the Republican Party convention. This was where the party was gathering to debate policy, make connections and ultimately choose Richard Nixon to be their nominee for the upcoming presidential election. Bundy was intoxicated by that environment of wealth and influence and found that he could navigate it quite successfully. He was able to rub shoulders with the kinds of rich and powerful men that he aspired to become and to learn how they moved through the world. National politics, with all its skullduggery and doublespeak, felt strangely familiar for a man like Ted who lived his whole life disguising his true feelings and always saying what he thought others wanted to hear. He felt accepted there, part of the establishment. Watching Senator Richard Nixon on his path to the presidency was inspiring, and Ted Bundy finally felt that, after years of wandering aimlessly, he had landed in the career where he belonged.

Back home in Seattle, and despite his starry-eyed political aspirations, the reality of his life was very different. The romance with Diane had grown stale and unsatisfying, no matter how hard he tried to recapture their glory days. His parade of menial jobs, his disinterest in anything academic, as well as a worrying lack of ambition and direction did not inspire confidence in Diane that her boyfriend would be able to give her the kind of charmed life that she had grown up with and that she expected in the future.

Diane graduated in the spring of 1968 and promptly accepted a job offer in San Francisco, 800 miles away from Ted. They told each other that the separation would only be temporary and that they would keep in touch by writing letters all the time, but it wasn't very long before her letters became bland and forced, and then she simply stopped writing altogether.

Bundy was heartbroken. With no better prospects emerging in Seattle, he decided to risk it all for love. He packed up his few belongings and headed off down to San Francisco in a desperate attempt to rekindle the romance that had shaped his young life. But it was not to be. Out of the college context and back in California, Diane had moved on from her college romance. When she looked at Ted, she found him to be "very emotional and unsure of himself", according to Ann Rule. He was simply not the man that she had thought he was. In fact, Diane "had a niggling suspicion that he used people, that he would become close to people who might do favours for him, and that he took advantage of them".

They tried to keep up appearances for a few months but eventually Diane told Ted in no uncertain terms that the relationship was over between them and that it was time for him to move on.

"This was my main criticism of him after the year and a half of our relationship," she said. "He wasn't strong. He wasn't real masculine. If I got mad at him because he did something he sort of felt apologetic about it. He wouldn't stand up for himself."

Bundy could not have been surprised by this turn of events. He must have known that he was falling short of Diane's high standards. Later on, he freely admitted, "I experienced any number of insecurities with Diane. There were occasions when I felt she expected a great deal more from me than I was really capable of giving. I was not in a position to take her out and squire her around in the manner in which she was accustomed. She didn't understand what I was going through."

But just because it wasn't exactly a surprise doesn't mean that he was not devastated by the end of the relationship. He had built his whole world around this woman, and in his mind, she was his ticket to the kind of life that he thought he deserved. All of that went away, along with the relationship. The life he had begun to imagine for himself in the upper echelons of society had been built on flimsy foundations, like a sandcastle washed away by the rising tide. In the days and weeks that followed, he spent his waking hours analyzing the relationship, trying to understand where it had all gone wrong. For the first time, Bundy began to understand that his access to "normal", upper-middle class society was not guaranteed, and that it was entirely dependent on other people. It merely reinforced to him the idea that he was different from the kinds of people that he idolized.

Bundy had been aware that his commitment to Diane, which even he knew was stronger than her commitment to him, would be enough to carry them through.

Being unceremoniously dumped by his first girlfriend had a profound impact on his life. Many people who study Bundy's psychology believe it was the moment where it all changed for him, the catalyst that sparked major changes in his personality and reshaped how he thought about himself. Rejection fuelled a raging resentment towards Diane and women who looked like her, and this underlying resentment only grew over time, eventually pushing him towards more and more extreme criminal behaviour in his later years.

"I had this overwhelming sense of rejection," he remembered. "Not just her but everything."

Detailed records of that time in Ted Bundy's life are hard to come by. It seems he spent the next few months wandering through the world in a daze, trying to make sense of who he was and what he was supposed to be doing with his life. "The tail end of that summer is really a blank. I mean, it was a nightmare for me. I have no idea what the hell I did," he said.

What is known is that in 1969, Ted left California in his beloved VW Beetle on a road trip across the country with no clear destination or goal other than to get away from the site of his deepest rejection and to attempt a reinvention. He travelled east into Colorado, stayed for a while and then kept going. He is known to have visited a few relatives in Arkansas before continuing east, eventually ending up back in Philadelphia where he lived as a small child with the only man he had ever really respected, Samuel Cowell.

Something must have clicked for him back in Philadelphia. Perhaps there was finally a sense of belonging among the Cowells, many of whom were artists, writers and teachers. Once again, on an impulse, he decided he would be staying on the east coast, and so he enrolled at Temple University and resumed his seemingly endless quest to earn a university degree.

But that chapter of his life had barely begun before Bundy discovered the shocking news about his real parentage that had been hidden for so long. The details of how he found out are unclear. One source suggested that while he was back in Philadelphia with his extended family, a cousin began to tease Ted about the fact that his "sister" was actually his mother. When he denied something so ridiculous, the cousin insisted and told him to go and find his birth certificate if he really wanted to know the truth. Bundy tried to laugh it off, but when he was alone in his childhood home, he began to search and search until he found the birth certificate and received the shocking confirmation that his mother was listed as Eleanor Louise Cowell and that his father was a man he had never heard of called Lloyd Marshall. On top of that revelation came another one – the couple he had thought of as his parents his whole life were actually his grandparents.

Once again, just like when Diane rejected him, Ted Bundy's entire identity was called into question.

The enormous well of resentment that he had built up towards his mother over the years burst its wall and became something that truly shaped his personality. He could not believe that she had not had the decency to tell him herself, and that she would leave him open to ridicule from the cousins who knew something about his life that he knew nothing about. This revelation, coupled with the break-up, made 1969 a pivotal year in the life of Ted Bundy, and only served to pour rocket fuel on his sense of isolation and resentment that would only keep growing over the next few years.

After only a few weeks at Temple University, Ted dropped out and made his way back to Seattle, where he re-enrolled at the University of Washington, this time with a plan to study psychology. Perhaps he reasoned that this field of study would help him understand his feelings better and give him answers as to why his mother would have lied to him like that.

Back on the west coast, he started to frequent many of the places where he had enjoyed the happiest moments of his life with Diane. He tried desperately to recapture that feeling of promise and destiny, but it was unavailable to him. His feelings of sadness and heartbreak about Diane began to metastasize into a desire for revenge. He reasoned that it was only fair that Diane should pay for making him feel so miserable and ruining his life. It was her fault that his life had fallen apart, and why should she get to live such a happy life when she had made him so miserable? Ted began to think up elaborate ways to get back at her. His greatest desire was to make her see what she had given up when she turned her back on him. He decided that the way he was going to do that was to become the kind of man that Diane had given up thinking he could be, so she would regret ever breaking up with him.

For these reasons, he was grateful to have found psychology as an arena of study, after having failed profoundly at all his other academic pursuits. He could use it to pursue his goals. Studying psychology gave him a deeper, more rounded insight into human behaviour and emotions, which he could manipulate to his advantage. Bundy learned about psychological vulnerabilities, allowing him to more effectively target and lure his victims. It also aided him in maintaining his facade of normality. Despite whatever he was feeling, he could learn to mimic expected behaviours and emotions and blend in with society even as he broke all of its rules.

Not only were these useful tools that he would use to entrap his future victims, but they also provided a framework for rationalizing his own deviant thoughts and behaviours, potentially fuelling his narcissism and sense of intellectual superiority.

In the early '70s, he threw himself into his studies in a way that he never had before and settled into campus life. While he still thought about Diane all the time, there was no shortage of pretty young women with dark hair parted down the middle. Ted knew his type, and he was surrounded by them on campus.

During that period of rebuilding his shattered ego, a young woman called Liz Kloepfer entered his life and would become central to the next bloody chapter that was about to be written.

4

A Normal Life with Liz

In the fall of 1969, Ted Bundy was back at the University of Washington in a third attempt to earn a college degree. This time, as mentioned earlier, he was enrolled to study psychology and, for the first time in his life, he found himself engaged with the coursework. By studying the human mind, he was better able to understand the complexities of human behaviour and personality. Did it help him to master his own emotions and rationalize his behaviour? Did it help him understand how to win over people's trust using charm and likeability? There was one particular experiment that he was able to use over and over again. During a class, the professor asked the students to run an experiment on whether or not people are more trusting towards a stranger if the person asking for help appeared disabled, for example if they are using crutches to walk or wearing a cast on an arm. Bundy liked the results of this experiment so much that he began to use it to his advantage when attempting to coerce women to follow him somewhere secluded. One of his most effective ploys to isolate his young victims was to wear a fake cast on an arm or leg, and then ask them to help him carry something to the car because he couldn't manage on his own.

As the '60s drew to a close, Ted was still suffering the effects of depression following the big break-up with Diane. One night, he decided to quit the books and go grab a beer at the well-known Sandpiper Tavern in the University District. The Seattle neighbourhood had a fun, casual and youthful atmosphere, thanks to the presence of the university campus and the many students who lived in the various dorms and frat houses in the area.

Bundy tried to be upbeat and fit in, but he wasn't feeling cheerful or sociable at all. So he ordered a beer and sat down alone, wondering what Diane was up to, who she was seeing now, and replaying all the mistakes he had made in the relationship over and over again in his mind. He barely noticed a young woman sitting a few stools down the bar from him who was being aggressively "chatted up" by a drunk and over-enthusiastic patron. If Ted had been paying attention, he would have seen from her body language that the situation was making her very uncomfortable.

Eventually, the young woman, Liz Kloepfer, decided to do something about it. She got up, made an excuse to the man, and walked directly over to sit next to Ted Bundy. She remembers later that he looked sad, quiet and vulnerable – the complete opposite traits of the man she was trying to escape. "You look like your best friend just died," she said to him, with one eye still on the man she was trying to escape. When Ted looked up, he saw a pretty, young 24-year-old woman standing over him. He asked her to sit down, and they began chatting. She introduced herself and Bundy was intrigued. He managed to get her talking, and soon she had told him all about her life: how she was working as a secretary at the University of Washington Medical School, how difficult it had been moving to Seattle from Utah and how she never normally went out to bars as she had a young daughter and could not afford the cost of a babysitter.

That night, Bundy behaved like a total gentleman. He was engaging, courteous and funny. With his boyish good looks and knack for saying the right thing, Liz was smitten straight away. They talked for hours that night, and shortly before the Sandpiper closed, she invited him to stay over at her place. They walked through the dark to her apartment. She paid the babysitter, who left shortly afterwards, and she implored Bundy to keep his voice down as her daughter, Molly, was fast asleep.

That night, Bundy ended up sleeping over at Liz's place. They talked, laughed and bonded until the early hours. That night between them was platonic but it didn't stay that way, and Bundy found that he was as intrigued by her as she was by him. They kept on seeing each other, and it didn't take long for a relationship between Ted and Liz to blossom. He was exactly the kind of person that she had been hoping to meet – kind, sophisticated and clearly on a path to success.

In her book written many years later, Liz Kloepfer admits, "I handed Ted my life and said, 'Here. Take care of me.' He did in a lot of ways, but I became more and more dependent upon him. When I felt his love, I was on top of the world; when I felt nothing from Ted, I felt that I was nothing."

It wasn't long before Ted gave up his drab accommodation and moved into Liz's homely apartment. Liz was delighted that Molly seemed to adore Ted as much as she did. Within a few weeks, they had formed a small, tight-knit family unit. Ted became the father Molly had never had. He was fun, playful and good to her mother. Family photos from those years show a happy, boisterous little trio going out on picnics, riding horses, goofing around and sharing lots of special moments together as a family. "This was a whole new dimension to living that I had never seen before," he admitted to journalist Stephen Michaud.

In various later interviews, Liz described how Ted took them to his favourite restaurant and rug store, how he made rain with the sprinkler while Molly and her friends ran through it holding umbrellas, how Bundy taught Molly to ride a bike and made her giggle at bedtime by messing up the words of the books he read her … in other words, many of the fun things that one might experience growing up with a father who had a healthy mind.

"I completely trusted him," she would later say in interviews, with Liz saying he was a complete gentleman and that her parents loved him.

But in February of 1970, something happened that provided Liz a glimpse of a darker side to her partner that she had not previously been aware of. It all started off so joyfully and was a direct result of Liz being so very much in love with Ted. She came home one day and announced that she no longer wanted to call him her "boyfriend Ted"; she had decided that she wanted to call him her "husband Ted".

Bundy was flattered and delighted. He promptly borrowed $5 from a friend, took Liz by the hand, and they hurried off down to the courthouse to get married. The young couple standing before the magistrate with little to their names other than hopes and dreams of a better life would have appeared no different to any other couple taking that bold step together and cementing their union. Liz was strategic about her love for Ted, and she realized that many people in her life would wonder why she had married a man she barely knew. She decided that it would be a good idea not to tell her parents yet that she had married a student who she had met in a bar only a few months earlier.

Ted was oblivious to the fact that she was hiding him, until she sheepishly admitted that her mom and dad were coming to Seattle to visit her and asked Ted if he would mind moving all of his things out of the apartment for a few days in order not to upset her very conservative parents.

She was used to the easygoing, affable Ted and expected him to shrug and say, "No problem." But what she got was

43

something else entirely. His face was flooded by a cold, distant look she had never seen before. He acted as if he had been mortally wounded, picking up the marriage certificate they had just obtained and tearing it into a million pieces, before flinging it on to the floor and shaming Liz by shouting, "If you're that hung up on what your parents think, then you're not ready to get married!"

She was stunned and sorry, and the storm passed within a few days. Bundy reverted back to his old, pleasant self, but from that moment on, she made a note to remember that there were darker currents within Ted Bundy than she had previously known and that she should not take his pleasant attitude for granted.

For the first few years, these incidents that showed his dark side were few and far between. Bundy played the part of the wholesome family man to a large degree, right up until the time when he became an active, regular killer in 1974.

In her memoir decades later, Liz described one specific incident when the two of them were alone without her daughter, when they visited a lake one afternoon. They were sitting on a small boat together when he suddenly put his hands on her back and shoved her into the very icy water.

At the time, she would later say, she did not take the act too seriously, as Bundy often appeared charming and playful. But what she did recall was the look in his eyes after he did it and the fact that he made no attempt to help her back onto the boat when she was gasping from how cold it was and trying to get out of the water.

Bundy was still studying psychology and was always short of money, so in 1971, he took on a job as a phone counsellor at Seattle's Suicide Hotline Crisis Center. He may have taken the job just to get him extra points towards his degree or to make some extra money. But there may have been more at play.

Of course, there is a huge irony in the fact that one of the world's most notorious serial killers would spend his days convincing people not to kill themselves, but by all accounts, Ted was good at the job and never stepped out of line. It was there where he met one of the most consequential people in his life, a former Seattle police officer and aspiring crime writer called Ann Rule, who would later go on to write one of the definitive Bundy biographies, *The Stranger Beside Me*. Rule saw nothing disturbing in Bundy's personality at the time; she described him as "kind, solicitous, and empathetic".

The job would have given him valuable insights into what people need to hear and feel in order to be persuaded. It would also have played into his burgeoning "god complex", a trait that many psychopaths have present in their personalities. Darrel Turner, a clinical and forensic psychologist who studied Bundy's case, explains: "There's this grandiose sense of self that comes along with psychopathy," Turner says. "This sense that you are someone special and that you are a powerful person and a need to feel powerful and a need to feel control, and so I think that working at a suicide hotline satisfied that need in Bundy, as well."

Alongside his work at the hotline and his studies, Bundy was still very interested in the idea of a career in politics. The year that he graduated, 1972, was an election year in the United States, and the position of governor of the state of Washington was on the ballot. Bundy, still very much a Republican, joined Governor Daniel J. Evans's re-election campaign. His job in the campaign machinery was an unusual one: he was assigned the task of posing as a college student, which was not hard since he had been one until very recently, and going to events where Evans's opponent would be appearing and making comments. Evans's opponent was a Democratic former governor called Albert Rosellini, and in the run-up to the election, Rosellini was a busy man.

Bundy spent his days going to functions, meeting people, shaking hands and making connections. "Here was something which allowed me to utilize my natural talent in politics and my assertiveness," he said. His ability to shift his personality to suit whatever company he was in is well documented. He had an innate ability to strike up a conversation, and with his good looks and easy charm, he was accepted without question in political circles. After investing so much in Diane Edwards in the hope that he would be able to move up in the world, Bundy was astonished by how easy it was to get into the inner circle using politics as a lever. "You went out to dinner with people," he said. "It's where they were. I got laid for the first time in Walla Walla. This life had always been missing for me and now here it was."

Whenever Rosellini started speaking, Ted would stop what he was doing, record the speeches and then deliver them to Governor Evans's office for analysis. Eventually, his activities drew suspicion and the Democratic hosts at these events figured out what he was doing. It was hardly a crime, but in the aftermath of the Watergate scandal, the story of the "spying" campaign in Seattle made TV news headlines. There's a clip of Ted Bundy appearing on national television to talk about his work for the Evans campaign. He managed to minimize what he was doing, acting demure and saying, "It's hard for me to believe that what I did was newsworthy. My part in this campaign is so insignificant that I'm embarrassed I should be getting this publicity from it." But that was a far cry from the truth. In fact, Bundy wasn't embarrassed by all the attention. On the contrary, he loved it and couldn't get enough of being in the spotlight.

When Governor Evans was re-elected later that year, Bundy was thrilled. It meant that he would most likely move up in the ranks of the local Republican Party. Soon enough, he was hired as an assistant to Ross Davis, Chairman of the Washington State Republican Party. Davis had high confidence in Bundy and liked the fact that he was "smart, aggressive … and a believer in the system."

But beneath this polished exterior of political success, Bundy was still nursing old wounds. Despite his rising status and newfound connections, he remained fixated on proving himself to those who had rejected him in the past.

Thoughts of revenge against Diane had never really left his mind, and in 1973, four years after their break-up, Ted decided to put his long-nurtured plan into action. He was going to reach out to Diane, show her what a success he had become and try to woo her again. Of course, he told none of this to Liz.

The next time he went on a work trip down to California, he called her up and asked her if she wanted to go to dinner and catch up, for old times' sake. Diane must have been curious to see what had become of her ex, so she agreed to go. At the dinner, Ted pulled out all the stops. He was kind, courteous and confident and tried to portray himself as the kind of man that he knew Diane had always wanted him to be.

It worked. She couldn't believe how much he had matured and how well his career in politics was shaping up. The man sitting opposite her in a restaurant in California was confident, assured and knew exactly where he was going and how to get there. This was not the insecure, unsure-of-himself Ted Bundy that she had grown weary with all those years ago. This was someone she could see herself with, and she wasted no time in letting him know she was single and thanking him for getting back in touch with her.

Like he kept Diane a secret from Liz, so he kept Liz a secret from Diane. He made no mention that he was living with a woman and a daughter who viewed him as her stepfather or the life he had built up back in Seattle. The fact that she was living in California suited his plan perfectly. He was able to completely compartmentalize the various parts of his life and began to pursue two tracks at the same time – honing his skills of living a double life that no one around him would ever suspect.

While his career in politics was going well, he soon realized that he would never be more than an assistant with just an undergrad psychology degree. He realized that all the men he admired in the Republican Party had gotten law degrees from prestigious colleges, so that's what he set his sights on doing.

So in early 1973, he took the LSAT test, then applied to various prestigious law schools that would cement his rise to the top. His sense of self-confidence had returned with the re-emergence of Diane in his life. He almost believed everything that he was saying about himself and could picture himself walking the hallowed halls of Harvard, Yale or Princeton universities. Once again, reality and fantasy were unrelated. When his LSAT scores came back, Bundy was mortified to discover that his results were nothing more than mediocre. He remembers thinking, "I felt like I'd failed. Not only myself but my teachers and instructors at the university."

Luckily for him, the charm and charisma that he brought to his work were enough to convince a few of the prominent people in his office that he was a candidate worth investing in, and so Evans, Davis, and a few of his psychology professors wrote strong letters of recommendation that were enough to convince the law school at the University of Puget Sound that Ted Bundy was worth taking a chance on.

That was enough for him to gain acceptance into the law school of the University of Puget Sound starting in the fall of 1973. Having left in disgust at the end of 1965, almost ten years earlier, Bundy now found himself back at the University of Puget Sound, going to night school to study law. He was hardly thrilled at this turn of events, and his feelings about being back at

UPS were complicated by the fact that his mother had recently taken up a job as a secretary in the communications department at the university. For a man so obsessed with moving up in the world, it must have been a bitter pill to swallow knowing that he was back where he started and, once again, in his hometown and under the watchful eyes of his mother.

He managed to keep the rather modest status of his law school from Diane while he was still building up the image she had of him. Diane was under the impression that the break in their relationship had been good for Ted and that it had enabled him to get his act together. She recommitted herself to the new, improved Ted Bundy that she saw before her. More than once, she flew up to Seattle to see Ted during this period and made it abundantly clear to him that she was ready to take their relationship to the next level. Ted took her out to fine restaurants, showered her with attention that made her feel like, once again, she was the most important person in his life. In a sign that he was serious about marrying her, they even attended a few church services together. Despite the fact that he was in a committed relationship with Liz, he even had the nerve to introduce Diane to some of his co-workers and employers.

But, as always with Bundy, appearances were deceptive.

He still hadn't shaken the humiliation and pain of that late summer four years earlier when Diane had discarded him. This whole courtship was merely his plan of revenge being acted out. Having won her back over again with his charm and a newfound confidence, he decided the time was ripe to shatter her world like she had shattered his. And so it happened that late in 1973, and without any warning at all, he abruptly cut off all communication with Diane. Naturally, she was confused and worried. She kept trying to call him up and talk to him in an effort to find out what had happened, but he stonewalled her over and over again, engaging in a cruel and elaborate act of gaslighting. Every time she asked him what was going on, he acted dumb and simply repeated in a bemused tone, "Why Diane, I have no idea what you're talking about."

Eventually, she got the message and retreated from Ted Bundy's life once and for all. His long, strange form of revenge had been a success. But had this really been satisfying to Bundy? Probably somewhat, although it seems like a far more passive form of vengeance than what Ted would come to really enjoy in just a few short months.

By mid-July 1974, Liz was aware that Ted Bundy wasn't the perfect gentleman she believed him to be in the early period of their romance, but at the same time, not in her wildest dreams was he someone who was gaslighting another woman so completely, never mind a serial killer whose acts lay behind the increasing cases of missing women.

Whatever his reasons were for this strange behaviour, it's probably not a coincidence that his long, demented killing spree of women who looked just like Diane began shortly after he had enacted his revenge on her.

5

The Reign of Terror Begins

Washington State's weather is notorious for its gloom. Locals often quip, only half-jokingly, that the rain never ceases. But the natural beauty of the Cascade mountain range makes it a desirable playground for hikers. So it was that a couple, hiking in their favourite spot in December 1973, were expecting a pleasurable experience on yet another crisp day. And so, when they stumbled upon the body of a young girl at McKinney Park, they could not have been more shocked. She was lying face down on the damp forest floor. Her name was Katherine Devine, and she had last been seen trying to pick up a lift from Seattle to Oregon. The autopsy revealed that the 15-year-old Katherine had been sodomized and strangled before being dumped in the park.

It was the start of a brutal killing season for the northwest area of the United States that would terrify a generation of women and ruin many lives. Ted Bundy was never convicted of the murder of Katherine, and in fact, another man called William E. Cosden was convicted of that murder almost thirty years later. But many experts believe this was Ted Bundy's first kill, and it bore all the hallmarks of his brutal methodology.

Of course with hindsight, the work of a serial attacker has no distinctive beginning. It often begins on a continuum of smaller offences, like being a Peeping Tom and a shoplifter, and then ends in a secretive frenzy of brutal attacks behind closed doors. In the case of Ted Bundy, it is possible that there are unsolved murder cases that could be linked to him before the winter of 1974, but as far as confirmation goes, it seems very plausible that his first known victim, and one whose survival would prompt him to change his modus operandi, was a teenager named Karen Sparks.

She was just 18 years old when she settled into her basement room near the University of Washington in Seattle and, at the time, had the world at her feet. The university had grown in stature, quadrupling its intake since the 1940s, and Karen imagined herself walking between its red brick buildings and clock towers, green lawns and vibrant pockets of student life as the "Me" era of the '70s was in full swing. She had been accepted into the dance programme at the university, known for its modern dance and ballet, and was especially delighted to have three male roommates living in the same abode, as it made her feel as safe as safe could be.

On the night of 3 January 1974, with her registration at the institution done and dusted and her basement room set up just as she wanted it, she got into bed before midnight and fell fast asleep. But then, in the early hours of the morning, an intruder forced his way into her basement room. He ripped off a metal rod from her bedframe and began to savagely beat her with it, aiming for her head and striking as hard as he could. Karen had been fast asleep and now, in a matter of seconds, was completely unconscious. The attacker now used the same rod he'd used to beat her and raped her with it.

It was only much later, around 18 hours later in fact, when her roommates began wondering where she was and went downstairs to her room, perhaps expecting to find her asleep or relaxing in her room late at night. But instead, what the boys found was an image that would haunt them for the rest of their lives: there lay their friend and housemate in a pool of blood that had caked around her head, body and on the bedclothes. As they pulled back the covers, the full extent of what had happened was further revealed.

Karen was rushed off to Harborview Medical Center, where the shocked medical staff offloaded her from the ambulance and rushed the gurney to the surgical ward. Her parents received the call that no parent ever wants to get, and from that moment on, their family's lives were irrevocably changed.

Karen underwent treatment for severe injuries by a team of doctors and staff who were far more used to seeing young people injured unintentionally, and they could scarcely believe that this was the work of one human being on another, done in cold blood and for no apparent reason.

Little did they know that this was just the beginning of a pattern of killing that still had many years left to run.

For the next ten days, she lay in a coma with her devastated parents and sister praying for her recovery, and when she finally regained consciousness, she would be permanently disabled by the attack. Bundy had broken her skull, given her brain damage, and caused major internal injuries, including a ruptured bladder, with the rod from the bed frame.

Karen would go on to suffer permanent physical and cognitive impairments, including memory loss and difficulties with motor functions. After a very long recovery process, it became clear how permanent these injuries would be, and that Karen had also lost fifty per cent of her hearing and forty per cent of her vision, which would never return. She also would have to live with constant tinnitus (ringing in the ears) and epilepsy as a result of the attack.

Bundy, for his part, treated this attack as he would all the ones that were about to follow: just another hunt.

And, while this has been recorded as the first confirmed attack by a serial killer whose notoriety would earn him some type of twisted immortality in the minds of the public, it was Karen and her family who would have to live with the utter devastation.

She slipped out of the public gaze to live a quiet life that had begun as a young and hopeful dancer and ended up as a cognitively and physically impaired person.

It was only in 2020, some 46 years after the brutal attack, that she finally spoke out.

That year, Karen appeared in the Amazon Prime documentary series *Ted Bundy: Falling for a Killer*. This series gave her a platform to share her experience for the first time, decades after surviving Bundy's attack in 1974.

"I didn't talk about it because it's difficult to talk about. People don't understand the changes in your brain, the changes in your personality," she said.

For years, Sparks stayed out of the public eye. In the documentary, she opens up about the internal and emotional struggles she faced due to the assault's impact on her identity and cognitive abilities.

She said, "I don't remember anything from that night, which I am very thankful for. There's enough evidence in my mind that I don't need to relive anything, and I'm glad I don't have any memory of it."

She also reminded the public of how it affected her in the long run.

"I woke up about ten days later. I had to learn how to walk again and talk again, and I had to get back to functioning in society again."

This quote highlights the extent of her injuries and the long road to recovery that followed. The physical and cognitive rehabilitation she needed after the assault was extensive, impacting her life in profound ways.

On being a survivor, who became an accountant and started a family, she said, "I'm proud of myself that I made it this far and that I was strong enough to get back to life again."

She emphasized that she did not want to be defined solely by the attack, and her story would go on to become very significant as it represents one of the few survival stories among Bundy's victims.

At the time, the police did not link her attack to a serial offender, as they didn't yet have a pattern to follow. Her case initially seemed like an isolated incident, though the extreme brutality puzzled investigators. But later, as time unfolded, it would become clear that this was the first of such attacks on young women in the Pacific Northwest and later across other states. It is also believed that her survival might have contributed to Bundy's increasingly violent methods in later attacks, as he became more determined to avoid leaving witnesses behind to identify their attacker.

The attack bore all the hallmarks of what would become his signature modus operandi – attacking his victims as they slept and using extreme violence that combined sexual assault with physical brutality.

But at the time, 4 January 1974 simply marked the official beginning of what would become a reign of terror in Washington State and the day one family would be forever scarred by another person's base desires to cause harm and hurt.

6

And So It Begins

Early in 1974, Bundy managed to talk his way into a short-lived job as the assistant director of the Seattle Crime Prevention Advisory Commission. Not only did this role help him burnish his credentials as an upstanding member of the community, but it gave him unique insights into the ways that law enforcement and crime prevention forces did their work.

The author Stephen Michaud notes that this job "gave him access to a lot of crime statistics. He saw what the police did and did not do. And he saw all sorts of places where somebody who was smart enough could take advantage of the chaos and the lack of consistency from one jurisdiction to another."

In a particularly macabre detail about this job, Bundy was the author of a rape prevention pamphlet that was distributed in an effort to help local women stay safe. He was becoming more and more adept at presenting different versions of himself to the world, hiding his true identity from everyone but his victims. As he once noted, "It became almost like acting a role. It wasn't difficult. The more an actor acts in a role, the better he becomes at it, the more he is apt to feel comfortable in it, to be able to do things spontaneously. And get better, as it were, in his role."

Not only did Bundy believe that he was smarter than most members of the police force in the state of Washington, but he also had some insider knowledge that he was able to use to his advantage as he embarked on his reign of terror. Bundy said that he discovered that there were some well-intentioned people, but they didn't know what they should do.

That year, one of the best-known ski reporters in the Seattle area was a 21-year-old college senior called Lynda Ann Healy. She delivered the Northwest Ski Report twice a day – in the mornings and evenings. Winter sports were an obsession to sports fans in that part of the world, and there were over 250 miles of ski slopes to explore. The state's residents who took their skiing seriously would eagerly tune in to local radio broadcasts for the latest reports to find out whether they should be heading out to the slopes to ski.

Lynda was a slender young brunette with hair parted down the middle – a "type" that would later be revealed as Bundy's "favourite" type of victim. She was studying psychology and was known for her fun-loving and responsible nature. If Lynda said she would be somewhere, then she always would be.

She had grown up in a tight-knit family with her two younger siblings (one brother, one sister) and her parents. Being the eldest of the three, she had always been the responsible one. Family photographs show her lovingly cradling her little sister as a baby when she herself was only a few years old, and their brother sitting beside them.

Their house was in a sheltered middle-upper class community in a suburb just outside Seattle, but when Lynda enrolled at the University of Washington, a new era of her independence had begun. That's not to say she didn't continue to see her family very often after she moved in with roommates.

She was slender and with deep blue eyes, and though she was fancied by many of the young men on campus, she kept her eye on the prize: her studies, her early-morning job at the local radio station, and her efforts as a musician. Though she had an angelic voice and loved singing, her real passion was working with mentally handicapped children.

As a senior, she had moved in with four of her closest friends near the campus, and they enjoyed living a life where everything was in such close proximity. In fact, until the attack on Karen Sparks, she and her friends had absolutely no concerns about their safety and her parents never had a day's worry.

On Thursday 31 January, she rose early as usual, dressed warmly for the cold winter morning and cycled off to do her ski report. Next came her classes on campus, and later, sitting down to write a letter to a dear friend. She wrote about the dinner she planned to cook for her parents the following evening, and shared details of her college life.

At around 5pm, when it was getting dark, her roommate Jill Hodges picked her up on campus in her car and they headed home. After sharing a lively dinner with her housemates, Healy borrowed her friend's car and made a quick trip to the grocery store to purchase all she'd need for the dinner she planned to make for her parents the next evening.

She returned at around 8.30pm to find that her housemates were keen on an impromptu outing to a nearby tavern.

The name of this popular hangout was Dante's Tavern, and it was only a short five-minute walk away. They bundled up warmly and headed out. She didn't stay long because of her early shift at the at the radio station, but they drank a few pints and headed home, each heading off to their own rooms to study, read, doze, prepare for the next day …

At around 11.30pm, Lynda popped into one of her friend's bedrooms for a chat and was in very good spirits. They spoke about this and that, and then at around midnight, Lynda said she should head off to bed because of her early start, and she said goodnight to her friend.

Once back in her own room, she set her alarm for 5.30am, as usual, and made herself cosy under the covers. At various times, all her roommates did the same. It was just an average Thursday night and there was one more day of college to go before the fun of the weekend could begin.

Barbara Little's bedroom was right next door to Lynda's, separated by only a thin partition. She heard the alarm go off early the next morning then fell back asleep again. Thirty minutes later, Barbara woke up with a start and was surprised to hear that Lynda's alarm clock was still going off.

Eventually, an annoyed Barbara was forced to get up and go into Lynda's room, only to discover that Lynda was not there and the bed had been made up neatly, which was not something that she ever did before she rushed off to work.

Meanwhile, the producers of the Northwest Ski Report were beginning to get a little worried that their star ski reporter hadn't shown up for work. After waiting as long as they could, they eventually called the house and asked where Lynda was, but nobody was able to provide a good answer.

Regular listeners to the ski report, including Detective Kathleen McChesney, noticed that Lynda Healy was not on the air that morning.

After a few worried conversations, her housemates gathered in Lynda's room and discussed what they knew. She had not let any of them know that she would not be sleeping at home. Then they noticed that the back door was unlocked, even though they made a habit of keeping it locked. More worryingly, Lynda's bike, which she used to ride to the radio station, was still there.

The odds were not looking good: here was a dependable girl who never missed work, never left the door unlocked, never walked off without informing someone of her plans, and suddenly she was nowhere to be seen.

But even so, there were no signs of struggle in her room, so the girls were still hopeful as they set off for their early lectures that they would find Lynda and she would tell them a story about her night.

But by the early evening, she was still nowhere to be seen on campus, and when her parents arrived for the dinner she'd never made, the girls began to panic and called the police. First on the scene was Lieutenant Pat Murphy of the Seattle PD, who described the crime scene as "immaculate" and that her bed had been "made up neatly".

But when the detective opened the closet, a different picture began to emerge.

Investigators found Lynda's bloodstained nightgown in her closet, with the blood concentrated around the neck area. Curiously, the only missing clothes were those she had worn the previous night, which led author Ann Rule to speculate in her book that Lynda's abductor had removed Lynda's pyjamas and redressed her before carrying her off into the night.

A pink satin pillowcase and Lynda's backpack were also unaccounted for, and when the bedclothes were stripped off the bed, they found small patches of drying blood soaking the mattress. It was clear at that point that someone had snuck into the young woman's house, committed a terrible crime in complete silence, then cleaned up the crime scene and escaped with the victim's body, and no one had been any the wiser.

The police were on high alert, but almost immediately, they were thwarted by the fact that the assailant had made no mistakes and they had no clues to go on. It seemed that Lynda Healy had just disappeared into thin air.

At that stage, there was no clue at all as to who could have done that. It was only with hindsight that one could imagine that maybe Lynda fell into Bundy's gaze in the corridors of the psychology department where she was still studying and from which he had recently graduated. The young housemates also lived in the same part of town as Bundy and Liz, and perhaps most aptly, many sources would later report that Bundy used to frequent Dante's Tavern quite often and that perhaps he had set his sights on her right there and then followed her home.

Because of these various forms of common ground, it's impossible to know whether Bundy met Lynda somewhere along the way or if she just happened to be in the wrong place at the wrong time when Bundy was moved to execute his evil plans. Either way, the loving and warm letter she wrote to her friend was her last ever piece of correspondence. The dinner for which she had shopped for her parents never happened, and when investigators collected the letter as a piece of forensic evidence, they saw that it was so warm and full of life that one got a vivid impression of the young life stolen that night.

But for Bundy's part, Lynda was a piece of prey. He viewed her as a hunter views that which he seeks to catch, kill and notch up as another trophy.

Liz Kloepfer had been very disturbed when Bundy, as her boyfriend, had admitted to her one day that sometimes he liked to follow college girls walking around at night. He said he "would try not to do it, but ended up doing it anyway".

He had been a Peeping Tom since he was a young teenager, perfecting the "art" of staking out a secluded position from which he could see into a girl's bedroom and then waiting for her to come home and get undressed. There's no reason to believe that he would have dropped that habit back from his days in Tacoma, especially when he now lived in such a target-rich environment.

Lynda's tragic and mysterious disappearance happened just shy of a month since Karen Sparks had been attacked in her basement room near the campus, and at the time, though caution was at an all-time high after Sparks's, nobody had any reason to believe it was something other than a single and random, albeit horrifically brutal, attack.

At the first sight of the blood seen on Lynda's mattress, all that was about to change.

7

Every Month, a Young Woman Disappears

A month and a half after Lynda Healy's disappearance, another young woman was about to suffer the same fate.

Donna Gail Manson was a 19-year-old student at Evergreen State College near Olympia, an institution that could not have been more different from the University of Washington where Lynda had been enrolled.

While the University of Washington, some 330 miles away, had held up a proud tradition of conventional academia since its inception in 1861, Evergreen had only opened its doors three years before Donna arrived. It had quickly become known for its groundbreaking approach to education, and because it attracted students interested in non-traditional learning, it promoted a culture of creativity and independence. In other words, it was just the sort of place that a free spirit like Donna would be drawn to. She had the perfect mindset for its countercultural ethos and could not have been more excited when she arrived in her late teenage years to explore the world of music, arts and humanities courses that the college offered.

But though the college took such an interdisciplinary approach to its curricula, Donna, who was extremely bright, had her eyes very much set on becoming a professional flautist. She played the flute like a dream and spoke of joining a symphony orchestra one day.

But Donna's pursuits in tertiary education were hampered by her habitual use of marijuana. Although this natural drug was illegal in Washington State at the time, as it was in all states across the country, attitudes towards it had begun to shift during that decade. It was never hard for Donna to lay her hands on a "joint", and before long, her education suffered. She had also become obsessed with the occult and travelling around on a whim when she should have been studying.

She had developed a habit of taking off for no reason and would return to her friends on the campus with stories about her latest hitchhiking experience and where she'd ended up. Her roommate worried for her safety but was also bothered by her obsession with magic, death and alchemy. That same roommate was often called upon to cover for her in class when she slept in and didn't pitch up for classes. She also suffered from depression intermittently, helped in no small part by her constant marijuana use.

Despite her wanderings, she always returned to campus, and because of her love for music, her interest piqued when she caught wind of a jazz concert that was taking place there on 12 March 1974.

Tragically, however, her decision to attend the jazz concert would also cost her her life. At around 7pm, she left her room and headed off in the direction of the concert. She never arrived, however, and because of her lifestyle of going off travelling and hitchhiking, nobody thought any of it at first. For six days, those who knew her thought she had simply taken off once again to skip classes, explore the region, hitchhike and get high.

But that was not the case. With her dark hair parted in the middle, she fell into the ambit of Ted Bundy, who had spotted her before or on the day of her disappearance. He had then pretended to need assistance and had lured her to his VW Beetle.

She was never seen again.

With today's technology as it is, it would take a nanosecond for the authorities to spot a potential connection between the cases of Karen Sparks, Lynda Healy and Donna Gail Manson, but with Donna having lived over 300 miles from Lynda, the authorities only made telephonic contact about the disappearance of the woman, and at the time, no investigating officer spotted that a pattern was developing.

Like clockwork with his monthly abductions, Bundy would strike again in April. This time, the young woman whose life would be brutally cut short was called Susan Elaine Rancourt, and she would meet her end some 110 miles from where Donna had been murdered.

Susan was born and raised in a tiny town called La Conner in Skagit County, Washington State, where she lived with her family before attending college. La Conner only had around 700 residents in the early '70s, and so Susan had grown up in a close-knit community with her large family, in which she was one of six children.

Her parents placed strong emphasis on education and valued the importance it played in one's future. Susan took on this attitude too and had high hopes of completing a degree in medicine or an allied health profession.

In October 1973, she made the three-hour journey from small-town life in La Conner to the university town of Ellensburg and set herself up in her room at the campus of Central Washington State College. She was a bright and high-achieving student and was hoping to major in biology.

Apart from her academic prowess, she was also known as being sociable but rather shy, and she was very involved in student life, but this was never at the expense of her all-important studies.

She was so driven that she had worked two full-time jobs every day of the week in the summer before her freshman year so that she could pay for her own tuition. When her parents announced the family was moving away to Alaska, she was brave enough to say she wanted to stay behind to complete her degree.

Even while studying, she worked at a nursing home, had a very steady boyfriend, and jogged every morning and took karate classes. In other words, she was a very active and ambitious young woman who did not waste a single second of her time just lazing about.

One of Susan's greatest fears was the dark. She was always terrified that something dangerous could happen under the cover of night and never went anywhere alone.

But then, in a sick twist of fate, she faced her own fear and it cost her her life. On the night of 17 April 1974, it was midterm finals and she caught wind of an additional job opening up for dorm advisors over the summer. She had also completed interviews for summer work to gain practical experience in her field. She was looking forward to a productive summer and was eager to begin her career journey.

Being such an industrious person and also paying for her own tuition, she thought the added dorm advisor job might be an excellent opportunity to boost her income to support herself.

At around 8pm that evening, she carted a load of washing to the campus laundry and then took the brave step of walking to the advisor's meeting by herself in the hope of securing a job. Although it was dark, there were many students about, and she convinced herself that her fear of the dark should be subverted in the face of reality: it's a safe campus; there are many people about; nothing can go wrong …

By 9pm, the meeting was over, and despite a full and busy day, she had decided earlier that instead of collapsing into bed exhausted, she'd meet up with a friend to watch a German film. The friend was excited to see her, and as she waited for Susan, she had no doubt she would arrive – Susan was not one to let anyone down.

But then the minutes ticked by and Susan did not arrive. Her friend, thinking there must be some logical and fair explanation for her friend standing her up, bought her ticket and went into the movie alone, thinking that maybe Susan's silhouette would appear at the door and take the seat beside her.

Over at the laundry, another student was mildly irritated to find that someone had put their clothes in one of the machines but not taken them out again. The student removed the clothes and put them in a pile on a nearby table so that she could use the machine herself.

But then, the reality hit home: Susan had gone missing. She had disappeared without a trace or even a vague hint from anyone as to where she might be.

A massive manhunt ensued, but despite everyone's best efforts, Susan could not be found.

Her family had now joined the worst club in the world: parents whose children had gone missing.

A serial killer is defined as someone who commits three or more murders over an extended period, typically with a "cooling-off" period between each incident. Only with hindsight is it chillingly clear how Ted Bundy fitted the bill. The regularity of his murders in the first half of 1974 paints a clear picture of a man who needed around one month between murders for his twisted mind to "cool off" and to plot and plan his next one.

In Bundy's case, also with hindsight, it seems that this "cooling off" period entailed finding a hunting ground close enough to drive to but far enough away that the authorities in one county would not easily be comparing notes with those in the next.

And so, by 6 May that year, Bundy was ready to strike again.

Roberta Kathleen Parks, known by family and friends as Kathy, was an extremely beautiful young woman who was 20 years of age. She was born in Lakewood, Ohio, in 1954 and lived there with her parents and two older sisters during her early childhood before the family packed up their house and headed for the sunny shores of California.

But when it came time for her tertiary education, Kathy chose to enrol at Oregon State University in Corvallis, Oregon, very far from home.

After the ten-hour drive up north along the west coast of the country in 1972, she arrived outside Sackett Hall. This dormitory, with its red-brick buildings built around a quad surrounded by tree-lined lawns typical of the campus, had only just opened up for male students too.

Kathy unpacked her boxes and began a new era in her life. She was particularly happy that Sackett Hall was only 350 yards from the Memorial Union building, which meant just a five-minute walk would place her in the hub of university life. Restaurants, game rooms, a bowling alley and general public spaces for hanging out meant that the neoclassical building was like a magnet for students looking for some company and fun.

But on Monday night, 6 May 1974, shortly before 11pm, it was very quiet in the building as it was about to close.

That night, Kathy had been feeling very blue. She felt she was on bad terms with her father, albeit that they were a close-knit family, and was also struggling with a point of conflict between herself and her boyfriend, Christy McPhee. Kathy loved him but she felt he was pressuring her to settle down with him too soon, and she did not feel ready for such an adult-style commitment.

She sat down at her desk in her dorm room and wrote him a letter in which she expressed how down she felt, how much she loved him, and the fact she was going to take a walk around the campus to try to clear her mind.

She walked across the lawns outside Sackett Hall and began the five-minute walk to the Memorial Union cafeteria, where she hoped to grab a bite before it closed at 11pm. As she walked, she spotted a familiar face on the path: it was her friend Lorraine Fargo, who immediately spotted that Kathy was looking a bit downhearted. This was on a narrow side street that ran adjacent to the lawns outside the Memorial Union building.

Lorraine was aware of Kathy's issues with Chris and encouraged her to come to her room, also in Sackett Hall, for a chat and some comfort. Kathy said she would, but she first wanted to walk around the campus a bit more and maybe have something to eat.

Kathy then made her way into Memorial Union as planned, and as far as the evidence suggests, she likely stepped into the cafeteria to get some food just before it was about to close. One or two workers might have been milling around clearing up the restaurant for the day, but other than that, nobody was there … except for Ted Bundy.

It is likely he was able to prey on Kathy's emotional distress and offer her some fake comfort as he laid on the charm and acted like he understood how she felt. He then managed to lure her to his car and begin a nearly four-hour drive up to Taylor Mountain.

He would later claim that he raped her twice during the long journey under cover of night and then brutally murdered her on the mountain.

For those back home, the mystery was as maddening as this: Kathy was feeling blue, went out to the Memorial Union, chatted to a friend en route and was never seen again.

Perhaps Bundy's "cooling off" periods were getting shorter while his impulse to kill was becoming stronger by the day, or perhaps there was more calculation in his "one murder a month" modus operandi as 1974 stretched on with more disappearances of young women in the Pacific Northwest rocking the different countries in the region.

But one thing is for certain: on the first day of June that year, he was hungry for a hunt. It was time to rip away the life of another young woman who had the misfortune of crossing his path.

This time, the victim to meet a tragic and untimely end would be Brenda Carol Ball. The 22-year-old, in some ways, was his typical "type". Like many who had gone before her, she was very pretty, had dark hair parted in the middle and was very petite. She had dark brown innocent eyes and enjoyed nothing more than a fun night out.

In other ways, however, Bundy's move to hunt down Brenda was a departure from the pattern he had established thus far in Washington State in 1974. His previous victims were mainly studious college students aged 18 to 20 whom he had apprehended on prestigious campuses in the area. Brenda, however, was 22 years old and had been studying at the less "academic" institution of Highline Community College in Des Moines, which carried courses designed to meet the needs of the community. These courses were typically geared towards vocational training and transfer programmes to the bigger and more high-status universities.

It is not known what Brenda had been studying, but at any rate, just two weeks shy of the first of June, she had dropped out and was enjoying a lot of partying. The only previous victim who seemed similar in this regard was Donna Manson, who was also more of a Bohemian, free-spirited type than your classic college student studying in a dorm room until 2am.

Brenda was an only child and had graduated from high school in Des Moines, which is only 25 minutes away from Seattle. Her parents had gotten divorced and so she had not really known "family life" with two parents and siblings in a suburban house in the same way as many of the other victims.

She had moved into a communal house in Normandy Park, which was a ten-minute drive away from the college, and was staying with four other friends. She was fairly close to her roommates and chatted to them frequently, but her party-going and search for the next adventure meant that she'd often go AWOL for days on end.

On the last night of May 1974, she put on a funky outfit typical of the era – blue jeans, a turtleneck top, a jacket and brown clogs – and headed off on her own to a rather seedy club called the Flame Tavern located in Burien, just two miles away from Normandy Park. It is not known whether she had her own car or not, but it seems unlikely since she was often out hitchhiking and had also asked a friend for a lift home on this particular night.

Brenda had no problem going out to such a club on her own, and she sat watching the band with a drink in her hand and a smile on her face. She stayed there until the last round of drinks was on offer from the bar, and it was then that she asked the friend, who was a member of the band, for a lift home. He said he was really sorry but he couldn't help out, a moment that, in hindsight, could have changed her fate had she simply been dropped at home two miles away after the gig.

Instead, she was now out alone, intoxicated and with no transport, and when the sun rose the next morning, she was nowhere to be seen. Not in her bed, not around the house, not anywhere else.

But because Brenda was Brenda, at first there wasn't much concern. She loved nothing better than a multi-day adventure out and about and didn't feel particularly accountable to anyone regarding her whereabouts.

She had told her housemates prior to going to the tavern that night that she was considering "catching a ride to go camping with some friends four hours away at Sun Lakes-Dry Falls State Park" on the Memorial Day weekend after watching the band at the Flame.

And so, they didn't think too much of it that she wasn't at home. The only odd thing was that she had not come home to pack. Even a free spirit like Brenda would want to have her clothes and a sleeping bag and a few toiletries if she was heading off camping.

Even so, they thought there'd be a Brenda-type explanation – it might not be logical or what someone else would choose, but that was how she was living her life in those days.

But then as time went by, the roommates began to panic a little. Their first instinct was to contact Brenda's bank. When they learned that there had been no recent activity on her account, they grew increasingly alarmed and made the decision to call Brenda's parents in nearby Kent.

Now her parents began to panic too. Neither of them had heard from their only daughter in weeks, and it was clearly time to call the police.

Unlike the cases of previous victims, it was only on 17 June, two-and-a-half weeks after she'd fallen into Bundy's clutches, that Brenda was reported missing. But even then, the authorities failed to join the dots between Brenda and the other victims who had gone missing from college campuses.

No matter what happened that night when Brenda was in the clutches of Bundy, with the authorities at the time none the wiser, the most disturbing broader context would come out later when Liz Kloepfer shared her story from that very same night.

On that same evening, 31 May, Bundy had gone out earlier in the evening with Liz, her parents, and little Molly (Liz's daughter). The parents were out from Utah for Molly's Mormon baptism scheduled for the next day, and Bundy played his charming self, laughing and chatting at the table and paying for the dinner.

Liz had absolutely no doubt he'd be there for Molly's baptism the next day. He was, after all, her de facto stepfather, and the little girl had formed a very strong bond with him. As far as Liz was concerned, he adored her daughter and wouldn't miss her baptism for the world. She did find it a little disconcerting, however, that he seemed to be in such a rush to leave the dinner and appeared unsettled, but she brushed it aside, excited for the baptism the next day.

When the sun rose in the morning, the preparations began. Molly was dressed in her white dress to represent purity, the guests arrived, Liz's father was all prepared to do the actual baptizing, and everything had been perfectly set out. Except one thing was missing: Bundy.

Liz found it very odd that he was, seemingly, a few minutes late. But then time ticked on, and the baptism began and ended with no sign of Bundy. Liz was very upset by this, especially since it was making a bad impression on her parents.

It was only after two hours that Bundy came walking through the door, having missed the actual baptism and now arriving at the church for the post-baptism celebrations. He mumbled something about "car troubles" by way of explaining his tardiness, and that was that.

"Never in our wildest dreams did we think he was out abducting people," she would say much later in a police interview. But for now, she was simply upset he'd missed the big event, and she had absolutely no clue at all what the possible real reason was: that her boyfriend, a serial rapist and murderer, went to a tavern, picked up an innocent girl, and brutally ended her life for his own pleasure.

On 13 June 1974, just two weeks after Brenda Ball had been murdered by Ted Bundy, a local television news broadcast in Seattle led with the following story: "Georgann Hawkins was last seen Monday evening shortly after midnight. She had been visiting at the Beta House and was returning to her house just a half block away down this alley. Police believe she went along this route, and then somewhere she disappeared."

For the community of the University of Washington, this was devastating news. The campus community and broader Seattle society were still reeling from Lynda Healy's disappearance and the clear signs of foul play in her dorm room at the same university less than five months prior.

Georgann's disappearance was also coming hot on the heels of the four other young women who'd disappeared in the region, but up to this point, the authorities only connected the June disappearance with that of Healy.

Georgann had grown up in Sumner, Washington, with her loving parents and older sister Patti in a loving upper-middle-class Episcopalian household. George, as she was called in her close social circles, was a very spirited and social young woman. She was a keen athlete, swimmer and cheerleader, but also managed to maintain top marks throughout her education.

As a freshman at the university, she had enrolled in a journalism degree, hoping one day to get into broadcast journalism. She kept up her excellent grades, but there was just one subject that was bothering her, and that was Spanish.

She had joined the Kappa Alpha Theta sorority during this freshman year and began dating a fellow student named Marvin

Gellatly, who was a member of the Beta Theta Pi fraternity. Everything was going so well and she had the world at her feet: a great sorority, those excellent grades, a lovely boyfriend, a job lined up in Seattle for the summer holidays ...

She was scheduled to return to her family home on 13 June and head off for her first day at the summer job on the Monday of 17 June. But first, the obstacle of the Spanish exam.

On 10 June, she phoned her mom to discuss the exam the next day but then decided to make a turn at a party before knuckling down with her books again.

Georgann had a drink at the party and told a sorority sister that she was going to pop past Marvin's room to collect some Spanish notes that she felt would help her with her exam prep. It was already after midnight when she knocked on her boyfriend's door, and after a short visit, she left, holding the Spanish notes in her hand, and began the very short 350-foot walk from his dorm to hers. The paths were well lit and she had done the walk hundreds of times before. When she heard someone call her name from a window on her walk home, she looked up to see a friend of hers standing in his window on the second floor of the building looking down. They chatted and joked around briefly, and she walked off energized and ready for her Spanish exam prep.

She turned down the last brightly lit alley that would take her the remaining 40 feet back to her house, and she was never seen again.

Meantime, she had lost her keys a few days before, and her roommate waited to hear a few little pieces of gravel being thrown as usual at the window to wake her up to open the front door. But this never happened, and two hours later, the roommate felt truly anxious and told some other sorority sisters she was worried. One of them phoned Marvin at his dorm, but he said she'd left at around 1am, and he too now became very worried. The house mother was now woken, and she offered to stay up with the roommate waiting for Georgann's return.

But this never happened.

And only now would the police begin to join the dots not just between Lynda and Georgann from the same college, but also the other victims from the region who had disappeared with alarming regularity.

8

Lake Sammamish

Before one fateful day in mid-July of 1974, you would have been hard pressed to find a safer and more pleasant recreational space than Lake Sammamish in central Washington State, about 17 miles east of the University of Washington campus. Throughout the vibrant counterculture zeitgeist of the 1960s, when everything was changing, the state park around the lake – some 500 acres of pristine land – held its own as a more traditional family space.

Measuring over eight miles in length, the lake and its beautiful emerald green shoreline was able to absorb large numbers of visitors without ever feeling too overcrowded. As a result, it had emerged as one of the touchstones of the local community who came to relax on its shores, as well as a haven for sports and games enthusiasts who gathered from all over the state to swim, relax and play together.

The park offered a variety of activities that catered to families, young adults and nature enthusiasts alike and was, in short, the typical "slice of paradise" public space that also served as a social hub.

It was particularly popular for swimming and sunbathing in the summer months, and usually the weekends would see families arriving in droves and spreading their towels out on the sandy shores. Boating and watersports, softball and soccer – all these wholesome activities were synonymous with the park's relaxed atmosphere and what it had to offer by way of safe recreation.

Picnicking had also become a popular pastime there, and so the park was never what one would call an isolated area, especially during the summer months.

But even so, on 14 July 1974, it had even more visitors than usual. Rainier Beer, a popular alcohol brand in the Pacific Northwest, had planned their annual picnic there, and until Bundy arrived, it could not have been a more successful event.

It was a Sunday, and some 40,000 people arrived for the festivities. Countless cars had filed into the car park to deliver fun-seeking occupants, while many others had arrived on foot, bicycles and motorcycles. Wherever you looked, there was something festive going on: barrel-throwing competitions, three-legged races, musical bands ... you name it.

Families had arrived by the hundreds, but also notable that day were the numbers of young people who had poured in searching for some fun and to make new connections. Everywhere you looked there were groups of young women standing around in bikinis chatting and laughing, while men with long hair typical of the '70s cruised the shore in board shorts with no shirts on.

Janice Ott, a 23-year-old woman with long blonde hair and beautiful smoky green eyes, was one of the many young people who arrived at the park that morning.

She was living in Issaquah, Washington, just three miles away from the state park at the time, and had a bright future ahead of her. She was born in Spokane near to the state border with Idaho, 260 miles away from Issaquah. Her family were upstanding pillars of the community, with a father who was an academic and school teacher, and a loving mother who stayed home to raise Janice and her sister, Illona, who was two years older than her. Janice was an accomplished student, graduating high school with honours and participating in many school activities. She was, in essence, a social worker and "do-gooder" with a very caring nature and was given the nickname "sunshine girl" at work because of her friendly disposition.

Towards the end of 1972, she had married her sweetheart Jim Ott, but in 1974, they were living apart as he was completing his postgraduate studies in prosthetics at the University of California. The two spoke often and were looking forward to a romantic reunion.

In 1974, Janice had a job as a case worker at the Youth Services Center and was looking forward to a relaxing day off when she headed to the state park on the day of the Rainier Beer event.

On that particular Sunday, she got up, got dressed, spent some time at the laundromat washing her clothes and then enjoyed a chat and a cup of coffee with a friend. Once she had checked off all the chores on her to-do list, she found a pen and some paper and left a note for her roommate, which read, "I'll be at Lake Sammamish sunin' myself. See ya." She signed it off with a little picture of a smiling sun and then headed off towards the state park on her yellow ten-speed Tiger bike.

Not far away, Ted Bundy too was preparing for the day ahead. He pulled on white shorts and a white T-shirt and made sure he had brought along a medical sling for his arm.

He was still living in the University District at the time and had been with Liz for five years.

On the morning of the beer event at Lake Sammamish, he arrived at Liz's house to talk about the plans for the day and seemed to be gauging whether she would be at the event at the lake. She told Ted that she was planning on spending a relaxing day in the sun. She was vague about where that would take place and remembered that he seemed to keep pressing her for details of where exactly she would be.

Eventually Bundy left her house, perhaps satisfied that Liz would be at a different venue. He then started to prepare his sinister plans, and at some point later that morning, when he had everything organized, he set off towards Lake Sammamish in his light brown VW Beetle, sporting a fake sling over his arm that gave the impression that he had recently been injured.

The atmosphere at the park was charged with excitement. The whole space was alive with people and activities, and there were even more water sports than usual. In one section, a huge red banner stretched across the space with the words "Mountain Fresh Rainier" printed on it. Just in front of the banner, a band in red, white and blue symbolized the type of day it was: an all-American summer blast replete with music, merchandise, food and balloons.

The band members, dressed in striped waistcoats and basher hats, played their trumpets, banjos and drums in unison. Also filtering through the air was the sound of chatter and laughter and boats whizzing along the water. Not everyone took part in the games on offer, though. Some simply soaked up the atmosphere while sunbathing on towels on the sand next to the lake.

Almost invisible in such a big crowd where so much was going on was a lone man with his arm in a sling who seemed to be walking up and down, approaching various young women to elicit sympathy and asking if they would mind helping him for a few minutes as he tried to hitch his sailboat to his car only using one arm.

The first few women he went up to would later report the same experience: that a good-looking man approached them, had his arm in a sling, and asked for help loading a sailboat onto a car. Some of them apologized and said no at the get-go. Others, including a young woman named Mary Burr, agreed to help but became suspicious when it became obvious there was no sailboat near the car. Bundy would stammer out an excuse, saying that it was actually further up the road at his parents' place, to which those who had been lured thus far would respond with an apology and go back to their friends.

Another young woman, Janice Graham, aged 22, later told investigators that she had been approached by Bundy with this same story and described him as being friendly and seemingly sincere. It was only when she saw no sailboat that she, too, came to her senses and made an excuse that she was late to meet her husband and parents for lunch.

But Bundy persisted with his plan, and it was only a matter of time before two soft-hearted young women agreed to help him, which let Bundy take his dastardly plans all the way to their conclusion.

Janice Ott, like so many thousands of other women at the park that day, felt completely safe in a public park in broad daylight. She was lying on the beach alone, reading her book and soaking up the sun, just as she had told her roommate she would be doing.

Eyewitnesses would later describe how Janice, a petite woman of only five feet, arrived at the beach in cut-off blue Levi jeans and a soft white blouse. She found a spot on the sand and removed her clothes, under which was a black bikini. She lay for a while sunbathing and reading her book.

Bundy approached her, just as he had approached others, several times that day.

In broad daylight and in earshot of many other people, he walked up to her, introduced himself and sat down next to her on the beach.

"Hi, I'm Ted," he said.

"Hi, I'm Janice."

He immediately spun his web of lies about needing help with the sailboat and was pleased to see that this victim had a lot of potential; she was falling for his ruse. Eyewitnesses overheard him joking around that he would teach her how to sail and she joked that she would get to meet his parents when they fetched the boat.

The kind-hearted Janice soon obliged to give assistance, and it is clear that this time around, Bundy felt confident enough to say up front that the boat was not already at the car. She didn't mind as she was on her own, so she stood up, packed her book away, and wheeled her yellow bicycle alongside Ted, chatting with him as she went.

And that was the last time anyone saw her alive.

Because she had been alone at the lake, however, there were no immediate reports of a woman going missing.

It was not more than a few hours later that Bundy reappeared at Lake Sammamish State Park, but again, given the great many people milling around, sunbathing, swimming and playing festival games, he blended in easily.

Earlier that morning, a young woman named Denise Naslund had packed her bag for a day at the beach alongside the lake with her boyfriend, Kenneth, whom she had been dating for nine months, and another couple, Nancy and Bob. Denise was 18 years old, very petite and had a kind face to match her soft heart. She had thick dark hair that she had cut into a solid fringe typical of the era, and had dark smiling eyes, which she liked to frame with a thick line of eyeliner.

She was studying to be a computer programmer, working part time in an office to pay her way through night school, but on this sunny weekend day, she had nothing on her mind other than relaxing with her boyfriend and friends. They barbecued hot dogs, drank cool drinks and then dozed off in the sun.

While Denise lay asleep on her towel in a grassy area, a girl of just sixteen called Sindi Siebenbam was approached by Bundy with his boat story. She would later recall that he appeared nervous as he asked her for assistance. When she felt uneasy and said no, he became insistent, which only augmented her suspicions that this was not a man to be trusted. Sindi refused again and walked away, but not before she noticed him heading off in the direction of the restrooms.

Some 15 minutes later, a young woman named Patricia Ann Turner was approached by Ted, who now added a layer to his false story. This time, he said that he normally would ask his brother for help but that his brother was busy that day. She, too, felt uneasy about his manner and request, and she declined. Straight after that, yet another young woman, Jacqueline Plischke noticed a man with a sling staring at her as she locked up her bike. He then came up to her and tried the same story.

These various testimonies, when they were later put together, illustrated how Bundy had a single, determined focus that day, and that no matter how many times he got rejected, he would keep trying to find a victim. All the while, as he searched for his next victim, Janice Ott had already been kidnapped, taken out of the park and savagely attacked by him. At that point, it is likely she was still alive, but she had either been tied up or was too injured to escape.

It was near the restroom that he would finally find his next victim.

It was now around 4.40pm, but in mid-summer in Seattle, the sun only sets around 9pm, so there were still many hours of daylight available to those enjoying their Sunday out in the park. Denise woke up from her nap, got up from her towel and headed off to the restroom. She didn't say anything to Kenneth, Nancy or Bob, and they all assumed she was going to the toilet or possibly to look for her dog who had accompanied them to the lake and had been running around as dogs do.

Denise had told Nancy earlier that she felt a little "high" as they had had a beer and smoked a joint, so some people speculate that her guard might have been down when she encountered the charming Bundy near the restroom, which was only 60 feet from where they lay. Then again, she was widely known to be a kind person who would go out of her way to help others.

At first, her boyfriend and friends weren't too alarmed that she had been gone for a while. It was a day of relaxing, after all, and they were teenagers with few responsibilities.

But after an hour passed, they began to worry, especially when Denise's dog came back to the picnic spot without her.

By then, at around 5.30pm, Bundy had left the lake and had gone back to meet up with Liz. She had been half expecting Bundy to join her earlier since he had pressed her for details that morning about where she was spending the day. But that hadn't happened, and now it was time for supper and she was pleased when Ted suggested they all go out to a restaurant and eat together as a family.

Meanwhile, while he was resuming his other life as a boyfriend and de facto stepfather, the mood at Lake Sammamish had shifted gear.

Two hours with no sign of Denise turned into three and panic began to set in. Still, Denise's friends assumed something had happened but that she would still be found. They searched the park high and low for hours, but by the time the sun set and it got dark, they were losing hope that she was anywhere in the park. While the vast majority of people still there had no idea what was unfolding, it was slowly dawning on the officials at the park that something untoward might have happened.

At around 9pm, Kenneth drove Denise's car to her mother's house to tell her that her daughter had gone missing. Her mother immediately sensed that her daughter would not have gone anywhere without her purse and, even more than that, would never have wandered off without her beloved dog.

With her heart already shattering into pieces, she called the police and told them she just knew something terrible had happened.

She told an interviewer, "At about nine that night, I saw her boyfriend pull up in her car and I knew right then something was wrong and he said, 'I can't find Denise.' All I can think about was what her thoughts were and how long she suffered. Those thoughts are with me all the time."

Around the same time that Denise was confirmed as a missing person, people began to hear rumours that another girl, Janice, was also gone from Lake Sammamish. In the days that followed, the heady vibe of the beer event was replaced by a dark and sombre atmosphere that spread across the area. Missing people posters quickly went up and the news quickly spread across the police force, media outlets and public.

Reporter Ward Lucas was one of the first reporters on the case and immediately knew, from his background in law enforcement, that this was unlikely to be just a case of youngsters wandering off at a festival.

He had been working as a police detective in the area for years, but in the early '70s, he had moved over to journalism, where he was able to use his policing background to become a top-notch crime and investigative reporter.

"I was still at the radio station when they were abducted. I lived in a house just a couple miles down the road, so when I got a call saying get over to Lake Sammamish, I went over and began to interview people," Ward would later recall in the documentary series *Conversations with a Killer*. "This was the first time some really clear details came out."

As a crime reporter for KING-TV, Lucas was among the first journalists to cover the Lake Sammamish disappearances, and his interviewing witnesses and gathering crucial information for news reports led him to publicly suggest the cases of all these missing girls may be linked.

The footage of Lucas standing at the lake a few days after the disappearance stood in eerie contrast to footage of the festivities a few days before, and this captured the sense of doom that was holding the community in its grip.

Meanwhile, law enforcement officials were finally starting to draw clear lines between what were now ten missing women. The main driver behind this tireless work of connecting the dots was a rookie homicide detective with King County Sheriff's Office named Robert D. Keppel.

He, along with colleagues, was quick to recognize that Janice and Denise might be the latest victims of a perpetrator who had already struck several times. Keppel began investigating these cases, and over time, he was first to develop a hypothesis that a serial killer was at work in the Pacific Northwest. He began identifying commonalities such as the similar descriptions of the man involved and the nature of the crimes. But still there were no bodies to work with.

However, the Lake Sammamish murders produced three key pieces of evidence that changed the nature of the investigation.

Firstly, after talking to witnesses from the lake and gathering descriptions, Keppel helped to produce a composite sketch of the suspect. The sketch depicted a man with darkish hair, of average build, with a sling on his arm. This was consistent with multiple eyewitness reports, and the identikit was widely circulated in the media. Secondly, Janice Graham, the first woman who Bundy approached on that day, had seen his car, a tan VW, parked under a tree near the entrance. And finally, they had one other crucial piece of evidence to work with – a name. More than one witness had overheard the man with his arm in the cast introduce himself to women as "Ted".

From having almost nothing to work with, suddenly the police were able to throw themselves at leads.

To most people, these three pieces of evidence would have sent alarm bells furiously ringing, but Liz Kloepfer was still deep in denial that this could possibly be her Ted. After the Lake Sammamish disappearances and the sketch that appeared alongside the name "Ted", Liz's co-workers approached her at work holding the sketch. They asked if the suspect whose face had been drawn from witness testimony resembled her boyfriend. This was a moment that would come to typify Liz's confusion: a creeping sensation on the one hand that her boyfriend might be involved in the string of disappearances in the area, and a flat denial that he could possibly have anything to do with it.

Even Ted himself had to face co-workers who approached him joking that there was a killer with the same name and car as him, but his establishment credentials were so well established that nobody seriously thought it could be him. Ted Bundy was a nice guy, a pillar of the community, "Mr Up-and-coming Republican", as some called him. If anything, our Ted was just unlucky that there was a killer out there who looked like him, had the same name and drove the same car as he did.

But Liz couldn't shake the feeling that something was off.

She had noted that around the summer of 1972, he began acting differently towards her. For example, he would often leave her house quite late at night and say that he was going for a walk.

After Denise and Janice went missing, Liz asked Bundy directly, but in a joking way, if he knew anything about this man called Ted in a VW who had been spotted at the scene of the abductions. Naturally, he denied it, and she would later say she "didn't feel safe" bringing it up again lest she betray her own suspicions. Mixed into this was a feeling that he could only be the loving gentleman that she felt she knew very well. Her suspicions wouldn't go away, and she was unsure of how to proceed with this man who she still loved very much. Why did she find surgical gloves in his pocket one day? He wasn't a doctor. Why did the tyre jack in the car have tape around the handle? Not to mention the handcuffs she had found, and his current fetish of tying her up with nylon pantihose while they were having sex. None of it felt right, and so she eventually decided to put in an anonymous call with the Seattle police.

Her first words on the call were as follows: "I'm concerned about my boyfriend named Ted Bundy, whom you should look at."

After saying on the record that she was aware the interview was being taped and that it was being done so with her approval, she said, "He mentioned an incident about following a sorority girl. When he was out late at night, he would follow people like that. He'd try not to but he just did it anyway."

Liz had found very strange items around the home – a bowl filled with house keys, a bag of women's underwear, bandages and plaster of Paris. She'd even found a knife under the front seat of the car one time.

Again, with hindsight, it seems highly unusual that he was not immediately brought in for questioning, but she wasn't the only young woman who called in to say her boyfriend had acted suspiciously.

What he did fit to a tee, however, was the physical description, the type of car he had, and the right first name.

Evidence also emerged that this Ted had even been to Lake Sammamish the weekend before the tragic disappearances of Denise and Janice, and that there were no alibis for this particular Ted to show that he was definitely not at the crime scene on a certain day at a certain time.

This made him a prime suspect, but the list was still very long.

Journalist Ward Lucas recalls in *Conversations with a Killer* that he was invited to witness a late-night stake-out with the police.

"The captain of Seattle homicide had me do some ride-alongs with some of his detectives, staking out a suspect at the University of Washington," he said. "I was in the back seat of an undercover car with two plain-clothes policemen staking out somebody. We just sat there all night long on a radio, listening for any movement of his car, and there never was. And I didn't know at the time, in fact, didn't realise until some time later, it was Ted Bundy's car."

By then, they had a photograph of Ted Bundy, but this was not chosen by seven of eight witnesses in a line-up, and there were no fingerprints.

Basically, there wasn't enough evidence that could physically link Bundy to the crime. They had nothing to charge him with, and he wasn't even brought in for an official police interview.

This intervention could potentially have led to a different outcome and dozens of other young women's lives could have been saved. The story of Ted Bundy could have ended there and then, but there were other factors working against solving the case.

At the time, there were around 3,000 men named Ted in the area who owned a VW Beetle, a car that had become particularly popular at the time. Add to that the fact that Ted Bundy had a spotlessly clean record at the time, and police detection work was still very unsophisticated in the 1970s, forcing Keppel to go through the automobile database by hand.

As the weeks went by, the phones went quiet at the station as new information stopped coming in.

And with that, Bundy slid under the radar and was free to continue his reign of terror. But though he was not yet a suspect, the release of the composite sketch was a key moment in the investigation and itself became a focal point of the search for the man responsible.

Keppel's work helped inject a sense of urgency into the search for Ted Bundy. Recalling the days just after the Lake Sammamish disappearances, Keppel would later say in *Conversations with a Killer*, "When the girls went missing, our homicide sergeant assigned my partner and myself to the two cases. At the time, there were eight women missing in and around Seattle and people were pretty frightened about it so we set up a task force. That is when Kathy McChesney was brought in. We needed a female detective to interview females."

During that era, women in law enforcement were often marginalized, but Kathy McChesney quickly became a key component of the investigation into disappearances in the Pacific Northwest. She was only twenty-four when she was brought on board in what became the Ted Bundy serial killings. Her involvement began during an era in which her work was already breaking down long-established sexist barriers. She was the first female police officer to patrol in Washington State in 1971 and later became a crucial team member by way of interviewing witnesses and victims' acquaintances, later focusing particularly on Bundy's former girlfriends and female friends.

Her gender allowed her to gain their trust more easily, but McChesney also made major breakthroughs in the police systems of the time by strengthening coordination between different law enforcement officials.

This would prove vital in the case against Bundy.

But for now, it was the mystery of the two women who went missing at Lake Sammamish that was top of the agenda. The disappearance of Janice Ott and Denise Naslund would prove to be a pivotal moment in the investigation. The abductions occurred in broad daylight in a public park; there were witnesses who could describe Bundy's modus operandi and car; his first name, at least, was now known; and there was a police sketch.

But, tragically, with the authorities getting one step closer, Bundy had enough time to pack up his belongings and leave the state, not only to evade suspicion, but also to embark on a whole new series of awful murders on a new hunting ground.

He would later describe how he felt a "great weight lifting off his shoulders" when he left the scene of his crimes, but the devastated families he left in his wake had no such choice – their loved ones had simply disappeared, their lives had been permanently shattered and they didn't even have the solace of finding bodies to bury and mourn.

9

Moving to Utah

Ted Bundy had a sense that the net was finally beginning to close in on him. He was keenly aware that his risky behaviour at Lake Sammamish had provided law enforcement with vital clues they had not had before: a name, an identikit, eyewitnesses and a description of his car.

He couldn't believe how close they had come to catching him thanks to what had transpired on that eventful Sunday afternoon. The police had even put together a police line-up of potential suspects that included him as the prime suspect for one of the eyewitnesses who had seen a man with his arm in a sling talking to various women around the lake. But crucially, Ted's ability to change his appearance over and over again bore fruit. The witness failed to identify Bundy as the man from the lake that day, and so the authorities had no choice but to let him go and carry on their search for the mystery man. Still, Bundy knew that he had made a mistake and gotten lucky, and he was determined not to be so careless again.

In the weeks after the murders of Janice Ott and Denise Naslund, he kept a low profile while trying to figure out his next move. He had a job during that time working at the

Washington State Department of Emergency Services in Olympia, where he was an emergency management employee. His role involved assisting with various responsibilities related to emergency preparedness and response. The fact that Ted Bundy was intimately involved in the search for missing women at the exact same time as he was going out and killing them is one of the terrible and outrageous ironies of this story. It was at this job where he became friends with a young woman called Carole Ann Boone.

Like Liz, Carole was a vulnerable single mother with a great deal of empathy who was stuck in a relationship with an unsavoury man. When she met the seemingly worldly and ambitious Ted Bundy, they hit it off immediately. She told Michaud and Aynesworth when they were doing research for their book, "He struck me as being a rather shy person with a lot more going on under the surface than what was on the surface. He certainly was more dignified and restrained than the more certifiable types around the office."

At the office, Carole's co-workers regarded her as a friendly and maternal figure who could be counted on to do her work well, go the extra mile, and help out the less experienced employees using the expertise she quickly gathered there. She was slightly older than most of the others, and it was an open secret that Carole was regarded as the most capable person in the office. But she was also a fun person to be around, and when there were office-wide rubber-band fights or when office parties got out of control, the roots of the cutting loose could usually be traced back to Carole Ann Boone.

"She was a woman of great depth and intelligence and seemed to be, based on what Diana [Smith, Boone's best friend], said, really irretrievably broken, which made her vulnerable to a guy like that," said Trish Wood, the producer and director of the Bundy documentary *Falling for a Killer*. But in 1974, while

Bundy was embarking on the darkest period of his life so far, he and Carole were nothing more than close friends.

After dispatching Diane, his relationship with Liz was ongoing, but Bundy was restless and anxious that he was about to be apprehended. He spent his days waiting for a sign to point him in the direction of what to do next.

An answer came in the form of a second acceptance letter from the University of Utah to study law on the Salt Lake City campus. It was perfect. Ted saw a chance to escape state law enforcement officials and to conduct his lethal business on a new playing field where all the young women did not automatically have their guards up looking for the infamous "Ted" serial killer.

The only obstacle in his path was leaving behind Liz and Molly, but he placated them by saying that this would be just a temporary move across state lines and that their relationship was strong enough to survive long distance and whatever else the world threw at them. In truth, with all the quiet suspicion that she was harbouring in her heart, Liz Kloepfer was quite pleased to see Bundy go.

As he set off in his Volkswagen Beetle on the 840-mile journey down the I-84E through Oregon and Idaho, he would have felt a great sense of relief. Bundy knew that coordination between law enforcement across states was far from effective and that the chances of the net closing in on him had just slimmed considerably. At the age of 28, he was already an experienced killer, and so far he had gotten away with it. Unbeknownst to him, the state police were not as far behind him as he supposed. One more thing they did after they received the tip-off from Liz was to send a telex message to the authorities in Utah informing them that a prime suspect in the case had just moved to Salt Lake City.

Bundy took up residence in an affluent neighbourhood of Salt Lake City known as the Avenues, situated to the northeast of the city with spectacular views all the way up to the Wasatch Mountains and across the Salt Lake Valley.

It wasn't long before he met a young woman called Pandora Thompson, and they hit it off immediately. He struck her as being far more sophisticated than most of her local friends; he knew a lot about wine and he was at ease in French restaurants. The two of them began dating but there wasn't much chemistry, and after a few dates, they both realized that this was just supposed to be a friendship. About the one and only time they slept together, Pandora remembers almost nothing – indicating that it was neither great nor terrible, but just … forgettable. Unlike many serial killers, Bundy was able to have normal sexual relations with women that he knew and cared about. Those relationships never descended into depravity. He once remarked that he could not commit violence against someone once he knew them properly. That's why all of his victims were random strangers who happened to be in the wrong place at the wrong time.

The only strange memory Pandora has of the year she spent as friends with Ted Bundy was the night when they went dancing and he decided to keep rubbing his stubble so hard against her cheek that the pain caused her to walk off the dance floor and go home on her own. But never in her wildest dreams would Pandora have imagined that by this point in his life, Ted Bundy had already murdered so many young women just like her.

When classes began at the University of Utah, Bundy was determined to get his act together and prove to everyone that his LSAT scores were an anomaly and that he had the intellectual capacity to obtain a law degree and rise through the ranks in the world of politics. But that little self-delusional fiction didn't last long at all, and it soon became clear to Bundy that he was operating at a different level to the students around him. He even made a rare admission of frailty, noting that the others "had something, some intellectual capacity" that he lacked. The classes and the concepts being discussed made no sense to him. "It was a great disappointment to me," he remarked, and there is no doubt that his fragile self-esteem, which he had been working hard to rebuild over the previous years, was negatively affected by his lack of progress in the field of law.

Where did Bundy always find solace and comfort when his self-image was threatened? In heinous acts of violence, domination and murder.

On the second day of September, he took a drive out of Utah, crossing into Idaho where he picked up a young woman who was hitch-hiking. The details of this case are unclear, and her remains were never positively identified, but when her body was found, it was clear that she had been raped and strangled on a deserted road and left to rot. Shortly before his execution in 1979, Bundy admitted to the murder and claimed that he had returned the very next day to photograph his handiwork and then dismember the body.

A month later, on 1 October 1974, a 16-year-old girl called Nancy Wilcox went missing from the Salt Lake City suburb of Holladay. She was one of the unluckiest victims of Ted Bundy. It was a Tuesday night, and she heard a knock on the door shortly after dinner. It was John, a boy from her class at Olympus High School that she was dating, and he asked her dad if he could see Nancy. Somehow or other, the two men got into an argument. Nancy's sister Susie Wilcox recounts the events of that night. "We were watching TV, and Nancy was waiting for her boyfriend to come over. I could hear her talking to my dad, and he said, 'I just asked [John] to back up his truck. That's all I asked.' And she just goes, 'Well, did you yell?' She was hoping that she'd just find John because he just barely took off. That's all I saw, was her going out of the house, down the driveway. And then we didn't see her again."

She walked out into the night, looking for John, and simply disappeared. A few hours later, her family began to get worried about her. They called around to her friends and spoke to John's mother, but no one had seen Nancy. They were worried about a number of scenarios, including the possibility that Nancy had run away from home or that, worst-case scenario, she had killed herself because she was so depressed. Nancy had been having problems at home and at school for months, so this was within the realm of possibility.

The following day, her parents reported Nancy missing to the police. Her boyfriend John was certain that Nancy would have called him before she decided to do anything major. On the other hand, she may have found out that he had been seeing someone else on the side, and that could have been another reason she ran away. By the eleventh of November, the Sheriff's Office were feeling confident that this was a runaway case. Only her boyfriend John was more worried than that, convinced that Nancy would have told him she was going or called him from wherever she was.

Ken Farnsworth of the Utah Juvenile Division spent weeks looking for Nancy, chasing every lead he could think of and responding to possible sightings, but none of them ever led anywhere. She had reported a sexual assault earlier in the year from an older man, and the police thought for a while that he may be involved, but none of the threads they were following ever seemed to pan out.

Nancy's body was never found, but Bundy later recalled about the murder that Nancy had been walking down a "poorly lit main roadway" when he saw her. He parked his car, approached her with a story, then assaulted her in a nearby orchard before bundling her into his Volkswagen and driving her back to his apartment, where he restrained her for the next 24 hours. As far as he was concerned, she was nothing more than something the killer used to scratch an itch.

Three days before the end of the year, the *Deseret News* ran an article that summed up the situation under the headline "Teen runaways cause anguish." The article stated:

If you're the parent of a missing teenage girl, life is a special kind of nightmare. Doubts close in and you ask yourself where your daughter is, why she left and what she is doing. Along the Wasatch Front, another more frightening possibility has arisen.

In the past three months, the nude bodies of two teen-age girls have been found in mountainous areas – sexually assaulted, beaten, and strangled. Police believe they are the work of one man.

In Salt Lake City, members of the county sheriff's Juvenile Division have expressed concerns for the safety of 16-year-old Nancy Wilcox, who left her parents' Holladay home 10 weeks ago following an argument. She has not been heard from since.

October was a particularly bloody month for Ted Bundy. With no obligations to Liz and Molly to consider and no one at home to hide from, Bundy's murderous inclinations were unshackled and he was able to indulge over and over again.

Seventeen-year-old Melissa Anne Smith vanished on 18 October after leaving a Salt Lake City pizza parlour at 9:30pm. The police chief's daughter from suburban Midvale was found dead nine days later in the mountains, her body unclothed. Medical examiners made a chilling discovery: she may have survived in the custody of her killer for up to a week after being abducted.

Less than two weeks later, another 17-year-old met a similar fate to Melissa. Her name was Laura Ann Aime, and she disappeared on Halloween night, having been spotted attempting to hitchhike home after leaving a party shortly after midnight, 25 miles south of Lehi. On Thanksgiving Day, almost a month later, hikers discovered Laura's naked body in American Fork Canyon, nine miles northeast of where she had last been seen. The medical examiner determined that she had died on 20 November – twenty days after she vanished into the Utah night. Post-mortems revealed that both Laura and Melissa had been beaten, raped, sodomized and strangled with nylon stockings.

Wild stories began to circulate of a cave in American Fork Canyon, or possibly in Emigration Canyon, where the two young women had been held and tortured by the deranged serial killer. In later years, those myths were debunked, but rumours kept coming. After Bundy was accused of the crimes and they had a name to put to the killer, stories began to circulate of a small, dark cellar in the house where he lived where he would have likely detained his victims. A former tenant who lived in the same house as Ted remembered that "Ted had the only key to the cellar and [the tenant] said he heard Ted all the time at night slamming open and closing that door, and he could tell that Ted was down in the cellar a lot."

As his body count climbed higher and higher, Bundy grew more and more confident and brazen about what he was doing. The memories of his mistakes at Lake Sammamish began to fade and he seemed to operate under the belief that he would never get caught, that he was simply too smart for the police and that he was always going to be one step ahead of them. One of his routines was to always make sure to drive a fair distance away from the scene of the abductions in order to dispose of the bodies.

He had become overly confident in his ability to lure young women into his car in public places and trusted that no one would give him a second thought. It's not that they always took the bait, but his performance was always good enough to not arouse suspicion, so that they never thought about reporting him to the police.

On 8 November 1974, he pulled his Volkswagen into the parking lot of the Fashion Place Mall in Murray, Utah. The mall had opened two years previously with Sears and Nordstrom as its anchor tenants, and Bundy sensed that it would be a good hunting ground for him. After all, it was a popular hangout for young people who were still getting used to the availability of high-fashion items for sale in the state of Utah. On that particular evening, a shy teenager named Carol DaRonch decided, like she had so many times before, to head off to the mall to see her friends and find out what was new.

Unbeknownst to Carol, Ted Bundy had stalked her when she was on the way to the mall. He had seen her take the turnoff to the mall alone and park her car, and he had noted that she was alone and parked in a rather secluded spot, so he wrote down the number of her licence plate and waited for an opportunity.

Inside the mall, Carol was browsing when she was approached by a police officer with some bad news. He identified himself as Officer Roseland, read her licence plate number out and asked if that car was hers. When she said yes, the officer told Carol that someone had been caught trying to break into her car and that she would need to accompany him down to the police station and fill in a police report. Carol was initially sceptical and asked to see some ID, which the officer produced out of his pocket and flashed it in her direction without really allowing her to see what it said. "I thought he was kind of creepy. I thought he was a lot older than he was," she said, but she was also driven by a sense of needing to obey and help an authority figure, so she nodded and followed him out of the mall and into the parking lot.

In later years, Bundy admitted that he often drank heavily before an attack, and this time was no exception. Carol DaRonch claims she did notice the smell of alcohol on his breath but held her tongue. Her suspicions were further heightened by the fact that he was taking her to his VW Beetle and not an officially marked police car. She asked him about that, but Bundy, aka Officer Roseland, brushed away her concerns by explaining to her that he was working undercover.

Once inside the car though, alarm bells started to ring for Carol. First, he suggested that she put a seatbelt on, but she said it was fine as the station was only a half mile away. As soon as they took off, Carol DaRonch's misgivings turned into a full-blown panic. She knew the streets well and knew for a fact that they were not heading in the direction of the police station. Seeing her getting visibly upset and panicky, Bundy realized that he had no time to waste and he needed to make his move, so he pulled the car over to the side of the road and reached for the pair of handcuffs that he always kept in the car. Carol knew that she was in a fight for her life.

Even though he was also brandishing a gun and a crowbar, Carol thrashed around and managed to resist handing herself over. In the struggle that ensued, Bundy managed to get the handcuffs onto her wrists, only to discover that in fact he had handcuffed the same wrist twice. It was a critical error. "I was able to open the door on my side and get out, and he came out after me over the seat, and we just fought outside of the car," DaRonch recalled.

The pair began a life-and-death struggle on the side of the road. Bundy tried to bludgeon her with the crowbar, but she kept fighting and thwarting his every move. Just when he seemed like he would overpower her, a car began to approach, driven by Wilbur Walsh with his wife Mary in the passenger seat, who stared at the scene in disbelief. Carol knew instinctively that this was probably her last chance, so she broke free and bolted for the car. Mr Walsh screeched to a halt and Carol jumped inside, screaming for them to drive, drive! With the handcuffs dangling from her one wrist, the car pulled away, leaving Ted Bundy helpless at the side of the road.

He couldn't believe it. For the first time in his career of crime, there was a young woman out there who would easily be able to identify him as her attacker, and he had let her get away. While this was obviously a problem for Ted, it was not his primary concern. His real concerns were more urgent and primal. His bloodlust was up and he needed a kill. So instead of fleeing the scene and dumping his car, he drove straight to the nearby Viewmont High School in Bountiful, Utah, which was only about 20 miles away from the Fashion Place Mall.

Bundy pulled his VW into the school parking lot at around the time that the local high school theatre production was letting people out. He was still so hyped up with adrenalin from what had happened earlier that he needed to get out of the car and begin pacing up and down in the parking lot, as was noticed by a number of eyewitnesses who noted his weird behaviour. He was still confident in the fact that his police officer cover was good enough to get someone to trust him, so he started approaching people who were coming out of the show with the story about a car and a break-in.

Eventually, a young student called Debra Jean Kent believed his story and got into the "unmarked police car" and was whisked away to meet her awful and untimely demise. The 17-year-old girl was never seen again. Bundy took Debra Jean back to his apartment and kept her there for the next 24 hours, half of which she was alive for, before disposing of the body. When it was discovered hours later that she was missing, the police began combing the parking lot crime scene, where they found the key to a pair of handcuffs. That key fitted the cuffs that had been placed on the wrists of Carol DaRonch.

With so many abductions over the previous few weeks, it became very obvious to the authorities that a predator was lurking among them, and they remembered the alert they had received from the King County, Washington, police service. The news of missing girls in Utah slowly travelled all the way up the west coast to Seattle, where Liz Kloepfer was dismayed to hear that the killings, which had abated in Seattle since Ted left, were now happening in Utah, the state where Ted had relocated a few months earlier. For her, it was too much of a coincidence and just served to confirm what she had suspected in her heart of hearts – that the "Ted" killer was her Ted Bundy.

Liz knew what she had to do. She immediately called up the King County detectives who were investigating the spate of murders in Washington and repeated her suspicions. She was called in for a lengthy and detailed interview with Detective Randy Hergesheimer of the Major Crimes division. They were not unreceptive to her suspicions but were hamstrung by the fact that their most credible witness from the Lake Sammamish murders had failed to identify Ted in a police line-up.

By that point in time, the bodies of Denise Naslund and Janice Ott had been discovered, and the American public was stung by the brutality and sheer brazenness of the killer.

This time, Liz didn't just wait for the police to act. She was so frustrated that the Washington state police could not see it as clearly as she could that she put in a call to the Salt Lake County Sheriff's Office in early December and told them everything she knew and where her suspicions lay. The detectives there listened politely and added Ted's name to their list of suspects, but as there was still no credible forensic evidence to work with regarding the Utah disappearances, they didn't take any immediate action.

Later that month, when Ted called her up, Liz was worried that her betrayal of Ted had been exposed. But in fact, he had no idea of her suspicions or the fact that she was talking to the police. It turned out that he was just calling to tell her that he would be coming "home" in January 1975 to spend a week with her and Molly after his exams were completed.

Once again, Liz was torn between the deep suspicions she was harbouring about her man, but also by the love that she had nurtured for so long. She hadn't forgotten how good Ted was with her daughter and how committed he seemed to be to her. So she made up her mind to say nothing for the whole week that Ted was there to visit, and he had no idea that she suspected him. In a sign that the trip had gone exactly how he had hoped, as the time drew to a close and he was due back at college, the two of them planned that she would drive down to go and stay with him in Utah the following August.

10

Finding the Bones

By September 1974, the pattern of murders had been well established, and yet still not a single body had been found. The young women had been murdered with alarming regularity – one girl a month from January to June, as well as Denise Naslund and Janice Ott in July.

But August of that year was quiet, and the authorities breathed a sigh of relief as no young woman had the misfortune of crossing paths with this mysterious man who was notching up his murders like trophies and making life a nightmare for the people of Seattle. Bundy knew that he had to lie low; there was too much attention for him to carry on doing what he did.

It was also the time that he decided he needed to make a change and move on to happier hunting grounds.

This relocation to Utah would mark a significant change as he shifted his focus from the lush green of the Pacific Northwest to a more rugged, mountainous environment where he would later resume his criminal activities.

In the meantime, while Bundy was making plans to relocate, Janice's and Denise's families had been trapped in the nightmare of a six-week period, still having no clue what had happened to their missing relatives.

For the families of those who had gone missing earlier in the year, there was even less hope of a positive outcome.

Then, on 7 September, a cool and mild Saturday morning in Issaquah, two grouse hunters dressed in jeans, windbreakers and hiking boots were wandering around a heavily wooded area not far from a service road some two miles from Lake Sammamish State Park.

They were on the lookout for a grouse to snare and keeping their eyes close to the ground searching for these flightless birds when suddenly they came upon something that looked remarkably like a human skull. They stopped to investigate, and within minutes, they had found a stash of other bones as well. Shocked by their discovery, the hunters made their way to the nearest telephone to inform law enforcement officials of what they had found.

The police wasted no time in driving out to the location and began meticulously gathering the skeletal remains, ensuring that they carefully preserved any potential evidence related to the investigation.

No weapon was found at the scene, and no clothing either, suggesting that the victims' bodies were left there naked and unburied before animals (most likely coyotes) had scattered the bones around a wide area.

The initial examination of the bones was conducted by a team of forensic anthropologists, who assessed the skeletal features to try and determine age, sex and any other identifying characteristics. It wasn't long before their analysis indicated that the remains most likely belonged to two young females, consistent with the profiles of Denise Naslund and Janice Ott. But in order to confirm their findings, the most important analysis would come in the form of dental records.

Both young women had had specific dental work that was documented prior to their disappearances. Forensic odontologists were brought in, and they carried out careful dental radiography, particularly x-rays, on the teeth found in the skulls of the deceased, and this played a crucial role in confirming Denise's and Janice's identities. The radiographs provided detailed images of tooth structure and were able to reveal root patterns and any dental work done.

The presence of unique dental features that matched the records from before and after death proved beyond doubt that the bones the hunters had found belonged to Janice and Denise. What augmented the analysis was the fact that tufts of reddish blonde hair as well as dark brown hair were also found at the scene, and these were compared to hair found in the hairbrushes supplied by Denise's and Janice's families.

And so, by Wednesday 11 September, four days after the discovery of the bones, the authorities were able to state beyond any doubt that the bones belonged to the two young women who had disappeared just six weeks earlier three miles away at Lake Sammamish State Park. The very next day, residents of the Pacific Northwest woke up to the shocking story on the front page of *The Daily Chronicle* with the headline: "Bones are remains of 2 missing women."

But there had been a strange twist in the tale: along with the remains of Denise and Janice, another very limited selection of bones were found that belonged to neither of them. Initially, it was unclear whether these bones belonged to a female or male, and also the age of the victim was not determined at that stage. Naturally, however, suspicion grew quickly that the bones had to be from one or other of the six young women who had disappeared in the area that year and remained unaccounted for.

Explorer scouts were dispatched once more to comb the area and see if anything else could be found, but despite their best efforts, nothing else turned up.

For Denise's mother Eleanor, one part of the nightmare – the not knowing – was over and a new one had begun: the heartbreaking reality that her instincts were right, that Denise would never have left Lake Sammamish willingly without her dog, purse or car, and that she would never be coming home again.

Her family and friends fell into a state of shock, and the broader community had all the proof they needed that a murderer was loose in their midst.

The same was true for Janice Ott's parents, sister, husband and friends – their deepest fears had also become a reality. Each one of them would later testify that it was Janice's kind personality and willingness to help others that had so tragically led her into the evil murderer's snare.

As for the other skeletal remains found that day, it was impossible to clearly identify to whom they belonged. That identification, as well as the exact chain of events that followed Denise's and Janice's abductions, would have to wait over a decade until Bundy himself finally shared the horrific details of that fateful day in 1974 when he had ended the two women's lives and devastated the lives of countless others.

Six months and a bitter winter passed after Bundy's "dump site" near Issaquah had been uncovered, revealing the bones of Denise Naslund, Janice Ott and one other unidentifiable victim. The discovery had confounded the detectives working on the case and presented as many questions as answers. For example, if this was all the work of one serial killer and his "dump site" had been found, where had all or at least some of the previous victims been buried? Were there victims scattered in the mountains all over the northwest?

Their first answers would come six months later, in early March of 1975, long after Bundy had moved to Utah.

It was an overcast Saturday, cool and damp as is typical of the Pacific Northwest when the region is shaking off winter and slowly warming up for spring. On that day, two forestry students headed out of the city to undertake a forestry inventory project for an assignment. The two young men would be taking meticulous notes on an 80-acre piece of land on the slopes of Taylor Mountain that belonged to American timberland company Weyerhaeuser.

The two young men, Larry Sharie and Alexander Kamola, were not just fellow students but were good friends, both dedicated to their forestry studies. It was their second day on the site, and at around 2pm, they were taking measurements of an area when Alex suddenly blurted out, "Hey, look at this!" Larry came over to see that his friend was pointing to a human skull lying on the ground.

The two youngsters knew the right thing to do was not touch it at all, so they left it where it was, finished up their field work, and, after 4pm, headed back to a telephone in the town of Auburn. They told the King County Communications Center what they had found.

The police officers were surprised by this discovery and wondered if there was any chance that it could provide some clues as to the many disappearances that had taken place in the area during 1974.

Because it was so late in the afternoon, they decided the best plan was to leave everything as it was and head back there the following day.

On Sunday 2 March, the two young men provided the authorities with compass coordinates from their find and distances so they could pinpoint exactly where the skull was located. They also accompanied Officer Anderson back to the scene, and flagged their route so that it would be easier from then on to get more officers to the site.

Anderson confirmed their finding and later put in a call to Detective Keppel, who by then was deeply immersed in the many missing person cases that seemed to have dried up since he got involved. Accompanied by colleague Roger Dunn, Keppel set off in the fog and rain to see for himself. When they were around ten miles east of Issaquah, they exited off the highway and towards the site of the find. As they headed in the direction of the isolated areas that had once been Bundy's favourite jogging spot and the burial site where he discarded the bones of so many of the young women whose lives he had brutally cut short, Keppel felt the weight of the task ahead of them.

Arriving at the site, which was at an elevation of around 1,000 feet above sea level, the underbrush had grown thick with vine maples and blackberry bushes pushing up against one another. The foliage had been so thick that it was difficult for investigators to move through the terrain.

Writing his book *The Riverman: Ted Bundy and I Hunt for the Green River Killer* years later, Keppel would describe how they knew it would be tough as rain battered the car as they made their way onto higher terrain surrounded by dense woods on either side. Keppel was about to come face to face with the work of a killer he had been trying around the clock for several months to nail.

At the power line road, he and Dunn met the young Alex and Larry, who guided them through a maze of very wet vine maple branches. Dunn suggested it was unlikely that anyone would carry a body so far into the wilderness since the remains, they soon figured out, were over a thousand feet from the road. This still had to be discussed, but what was immediately apparent as they saw the skull was that it was without doubt human.

Worse yet, a large fracture on the right side of the cranium, which still lay on its other side just as the boys had left it, was clearly visible. A big piece of bone was missing, and from that moment, the sheer brutality and force of the killer's methods became clear.

But, aside from the skull, no additional bones from the same body were found nearby.

Keppel would note in his book how leaves from the previous autumn filled the cavity and how a spider's web had been woven over the jagged opening.

But most poignant of all was Keppel's immediate recognition of the teeth and thus, to whom the skull belonged. How many hours had he pored over photographs of the missing women and their dental records? And here he was, staring straight at what had become of Brenda Ball at the hands of a brutal killer.

The dental pattern featured familiar silver fillings that he could easily identify and which a forensic odontologist would verify just three days later. The men took photographs of Brenda's cranium from different angles before carefully lifting it up, ensuring that they made no changes to it since it was a crucial piece of forensic evidence.

A mammoth task lay ahead, but dusk was approaching and so they decided to return the next day to continue with the search for the rest of Brenda's skeletal remains. This time, a pack of six German Shepherds with their supersonic sense of smell would be joining them, as would their handlers in their orange jackets and blue pants, and another investigator.

All gathered at the intersection of the power line road, with the intention of meeting at the spot where Brenda's skull was found and then expanding outwards in search of the rest of her skeleton. But, despite the forestry students having placed markings of red tape on the trees, the dense and wet forest was a knot of foliage that all looked the same. Keppel soon had to admit to himself and the others that he was hopelessly lost.

At this point, the dog handlers thought the best way forward was to split up and head off in different directions and call one another if anything came to light. And before long, that's exactly what happened. Keppel heard a dog handler shouting out that he had found the spot where the cranium had lain, and as he tried to rush off in that direction, he tripped over a thick branch of a maple tree and ended up spread-eagled on the forest floor.

But this, it would turn out, was a lucky moment within the context of the grim task at hand: as he pushed himself up onto his knees, just four feet away he spotted yet another cranium, bleached by the sun, invaded by leaves and being used as the foundations for spiders and their webs. Keppel notes a poignant detail in his book, describing how a branch had grown through the facial bones while a six-inch radial fracture extended from its base.

Once again, the killer's dastardly deeds were imprinted on the bones of what had once been part of a beautiful young woman's face. That young woman, Keppel quickly realized, was Susan Rancourt, the college student who had been missing for almost a year, having disappeared on 17 April the previous year more than 150 miles away.

He would later describe in his memoir the twisted joy of finding evidence in the most frustrating of murder cases: "Without hesitation, I recognized the brilliant-white bridgework of Susan Elaine Rancourt, a coed missing since April 17, 1974, from Central Washington State College, which was over 150 miles away to the east. With embarrassing glee, I yelled to the others that I had found a cranium ... The extent of this killer's crimes was growing as more of the pieces of the puzzle came together."

He immediately called out to the others and was soon surrounded by the dogs and their handlers. Before long, the dogs, with their noses pressed to the ground, were making one find after another: first a single jawbone, then another, and then yet another. Now the investigators began making a master diagram of their findings – Brenda Ball's cranium, Susan Rancourt's cranium, and three jawbones. The remains bore clear marks of severe trauma, and in the days that followed, those on site steeled themselves to rake through every ounce of soil looking for evidence, no matter how large or small.

But the only additional human remains located were along an animal trail near a small creek. Susan Rancourt's shattered mandible was found about 800 feet from her skull, and it appeared as if an animal had dragged it off there deeper into the forest since the terrain was near-impossible for humans to navigate.

But most miraculous of all, given how dense the undergrowth of vine maples and blackberry bushes was in the area, was the group's location of a small clump of blonde hair. For those in forensics, this would be an excellent find, albeit an upsetting one that really highlighted the fact that this was a human being, a young woman who probably brushed her hair that day before heading out. The hair, analysts would discover, would turn out to be that of Brenda Ball.

A criminalist listed in the records as K. Sweeney coordinated the identification of the victims. These young women, who had once had their whole lives ahead of them, were now reduced to weathered skulls, sets of teeth, clumps of hair ...

Sweeney had the burden of contacting the personal dentists of the young women who had gone missing and then comparing images from their dental records with teeth set in mandibles abandoned in the woodlands.

After the scattered bones had all been found and matched to the young women who'd gone missing, theories emerged of intentional decapitation. Fortunately, however, these were quickly dismissed by experts due to the absence of neck vertebrae. Typically, if a victim is decapitated by a perpetrator, cuts are made below the base of the skull where severing vertebrae is easier, and in that event, neck vertebrae will be found at the scene.

This was not the case here, as far as the forensic evidence suggested. Of course, it wasn't impossible that the likes of Bundy would have taken pleasure in such an act, but the evidence was also stacked in favour of what the authorities wanted to convey: a sense of minimizing community fear.

All that could be said with any certainty was that Bundy had treated the site as his personal disposal patch in the woodlands, though of course at the time nobody knew he was the man behind it.

The name and identity of the person responsible were still shrouded in mystery, but at the very least, the findings at Taylor Mountain had contributed significantly to understanding the killer's mindset, activities and the tragic fate of his victims. They had highlighted both the challenges of locating remains in such dense vegetation and the importance of thorough forensic investigation. What they did not do, however, was provide the devastated and bereft families with any new information on the person behind these truly awful acts by one human being on others.

11

Colorado

Like Washington State in 1974, so Utah in 1975 began to feel a little claustrophobic for Ted Bundy. He thought perhaps he had pushed his luck in this state as far as it would go. But that didn't change the fact that he was feeling an insatiable hunger for blood. Once he realized that Utah was becoming too risky for him, he started venturing across state lines into Colorado looking for victims.

His search for new killing fields didn't take long to materialize. On 12 January, he happened upon a 23-year-old woman named Caryn Campbell. She was from Dearborn, Michigan, but was vacationing in Snowmass Village, a tiny skiing resort west of Aspen, Colorado.

Campbell was staying at the Wildwood Inn with her fiancé, a doctor from the town of Farmington Hills. Like Nancy Wilcox before her, Caryn Campbell's luck ran out at the wrong time. She didn't put herself at risk in any way – all she did was walk down the narrow hallway between the elevator and her hotel room at the same time that Ted Bundy was walking in the other direction. It's unclear how he did it, whether through charm or brute force, but somehow he was able to abduct Campbell, bundle her into his car and bludgeon her to death.

Her naked body was discovered a month later on a dirt road only a few miles away from the resort where she had been staying. The coroner found that Caryn's skull had been crushed by a grooved weapon, leaving distinct linear marks. Her killer had also slashed her left earlobe and carved deep wounds into her body with a blade.

Bundy must have been pleased with his foray into Colorado because barely eight weeks later, he was back there on the hunt for new victims, this time in the small town of Vail, 100 miles north of Snowmass Village. He had a new strategy to try out this time, which involved him hobbling around on crutches looking for sympathy and asking for help from sympathetic women out on their own. One such woman was Julie Lyle Cunningham, a 26-year-old ski instructor who was taking a stroll from her apartment to a dinner date with a friend. Like he had done so many times before, Bundy saw her, figured out in an instant that she fitted his victim profile and made his move. He approached and asked her if she could spare a moment to help him carry his ski boots to the car, seeing as he needed both hands to operate his crutches.

As soon as he had her alone near his car, he sprung into action, clubbing her over the head before handcuffing and abducting her, then driving approximately 90 miles away, where he sexually assaulted and murdered Cunningham, then hid her body away.

For some reason, Bundy enjoyed this killing so much that, weeks later, he was moved to drive six hours to revisit the body in its hiding place and inspect his handiwork. Interestingly, his predilection for revisiting the bodies of his earlier victims was the only time he worried that he might be caught. He told someone that if the cops had found one of his victims and set up a patrol car to watch the area where the body was found, then they would have caught him simply because there was no other reason to be in those places unless you had stashed a body there. Of course, that never happened because Bundy spent so much time and petrol money driving hours away to drop off and hide the bodies of the women that he killed.

By that stage, all semblance of a normal life had been abandoned. Bundy had dropped out of law school and was consumed by the demons that were driving him to go further and further. Three weeks after the murder of Cunningham, he was back in Colorado, where he stumbled upon Denise Lynn Oliverson, aged 25, while she was riding her bike to her parents' house. A newspaper article at the time reported that "police found Mrs Oliverson's shoes and bicycle under the Fifth Street bridge near some train tracks but have been unable to come up with any leads since". She had been married for a few short years in 1972, but that didn't last long, and at the time of her disappearance she was working as an assembler. Somehow Bundy had managed to get her off her bike and been able to murder her right there in his car, before dumping her body into the freezing waters of the Colorado River.

A month later, he decided it was time to switch up his modus operandi again. This time, he drove 250 miles in the opposite direction into a town called Pocatello, Idaho. He parked his car outside a junior high school and waited. Sure enough, a victim presented herself after a while. A 12-year-old girl by the name of Lynette Dawn Culver left school premises during her lunch break and was walking alone when she had the misfortune to run into Bundy. He snatched her and drove her to a hotel room in the Holiday Inn, where he raped her and then drowned her in the bathtub. Then he put her body back in the car and drove to the Snake River, where he disposed of the poor child.

Like so many of his other victims, her body was never found, and it was only due to a confession many years later that the authorities were able to close the tragic case.

Later that month, there was a brief respite from the madness and bloodlust and a return to some kind of normality when Bundy welcomed three of his former co-workers from Washington State on a trip to Utah, including Carole Ann Boone, who had come to see Ted for a two-week stay. They spent the days going skiing, staying up late and chatting about the good times they had enjoyed back in the office. There was a lot of reminiscing about how Bundy had been so popular among his co-workers, and they remembered the running joke in the office that Ted's car and name matched that of the famous serial killer who was terrorizing the area. It was still so preposterous for them to think of Ted Bundy as being that notorious killer that none of them seriously considered the fact that this mild-mannered former colleague, who frequently went out to help in the search for missing women, could be the perpetrator everyone was looking for.

On that trip to Utah, Bundy and a girlfriend of his, Pandora Thompson, took his friends to Salt Lake City's first and only gay bar, the Sun Tavern, during their visit. It was a bit of a risqué locale for a conservative town in the 1970s, and while the free-spirited Carole seemed to enjoy the experience, Ted reportedly acted uncomfortable and uptight.

Despite his long-term, long-distance relationship with Liz, there was definitely something more romantic brewing between Ted Bundy and Carole Ann Boone during the summer of 1975, and there has always been speculation that the pair became seriously involved during this trip. Of course, the romances with Liz and with Carole didn't stop Ted from also seeing other women in Utah.

Never one to stay faithful, and addicted to his secrets, Bundy had also become involved in a romance with a Utah law student as well as Carole Ann and maintaining his long-term relationship with Liz Kloepfer.

In early June of that year, he drove back up to Seattle to spend a week with Liz, and it went so well that they even discussed the possibility of getting married in December. She made no mention of the fact that she had been discussing him with authorities and he made no mention of the fact that he was having multiple affairs. Nevertheless, their relationship persisted.

By late June, all the niceties were over. Ted had fulfilled his duties and he was alone again and on the prowl for fresh blood. He decided to pay a visit to Brigham Young University (BYU).

Nineteen-year-old Susan Curtis had arrived in Provo, Utah, by bicycle the previous day. She was there to attend the Bountiful Orchard Youth Conference at BYU, which is a two-day religious gathering for young adults.

At approximately 8pm on the 28th, during the conference's formal banquet at the Wilkinson Student Center, Sue excused herself from the table wearing a full-length evening dress. She told other attendees she would be back soon; she just needed to return to her dormitory to brush her teeth – a quick walk across campus.

Sue left the banquet hall alone. It was the last time anyone would see her. When she failed to return, her absence was noted, but it wasn't the first time she had gone missing. The local newspaper reported Chief Kelsaw saying that "on previous occasions she had run away or disappeared for a number of days at a time and for that reason, he does not believe there has been an abduction".

By the time they figured out she was really gone, it was way too late. Despite extensive searches of the campus and surrounding areas, no trace of her body was ever found. The mystery of what happened during that short walk between the Student Center and her dormitory remains unsolved to this day.

She was the sixteenth known victim of Ted Bundy and one of five girls whose bodies were never recovered.

One of Ted Bundy's most useful skills was his ability to blend into his surroundings, and in Utah, there was nothing more mainstream than Mormonism, the dominant religion that was the very reason why Salt Lake City had been founded in the first place. Bundy began attending LDS (Latter Day Saints) services and dating Mormon women soon after he arrived, and in August 1975, he was formally baptized into the church. But rather than any meaningful spiritual conviction, Bundy's involvement with the Mormon church appears to have been primarily a way to blend into Utah society and appear trustworthy. It was yet another layer that he employed to give the appearance of being an upstanding citizen and to ensure that he was able to avoid any suspicion linking him to the "devious monster" that had been preying on women up and down the west coast of the country for the past few years.

As the number of victims kept growing, Bundy became more and more of a twisted master of methodical violence. He chose his weapons from the mundane world of everyday objects. He shunned firearms, understanding that gunshots were loud and drew attention and bullets left stories for forensic teams to read. Instead, he became adept at turning household items into instruments of death, favouring the quiet efficiency and close contact of blunt force and strangulation.

Before each attack, Bundy would meticulously map his killing grounds. He studied locations with an obsessive eye, identifying the perfect spots to abduct his victims and later conceal their bodies. This clinical attention to detail extended to the crimes themselves, and despite the fact that he was usually quite drunk by the time he acted, Bundy's criminal expertise proved remarkable – not a single fingerprint was ever recovered from any crime scene.

This forensic invisibility became his proud refrain during years of proclaimed innocence, a testament to how thoroughly he had perfected his dark craft.

12

Arrest

In the early hours of 16 August 1975, a tan VW Beetle was parked outside the house of two young women in Granger, a community of around 9,000 people living southwest of Salt Lake City. Their parents were out of town and the two girls were all alone. One of them, a 16-year-old girl called Kelly Gregson, was working a shift at a pizza place that night. All signs pointed to what lay ahead that night: yet another brutal murder that could be pinned on the catalogue of evil curated by one single serial killer. It might have been another heinous crime, replete with rape, severe head trauma and ultimately, a brutal murder followed by a callous disposal of human remains.

But on that particular night, as fate would have it, a Utah highway patrol trooper was in close proximity to the tan VW and was about to intercept fate.

That trooper was one Bob Hayward, who had served in the navy before moving across to law enforcement. When he joined the Utah highway patrol, he became the sergeant in charge of the Alcohol Safety Action Program. This was the first highway patrol unit in the state that focused specifically on drunk drivers, and at around 3am on that fateful morning, Hayward was updating a logbook detailing the unit's work.

He had just come off duty and was sitting in his car completing the details of the day's work when he received a call on his radio. A tan VW drove by and Hayward thought nothing of it, but as he continued on his way to help out with the call, he took a wrong turn.

This was the moment when he saw the VW Beetle once again, but this time it was parked outside the house of a neighbour. He happened to know the neighbour was away and that his two teenage daughters had stayed behind in the city to look after the family home.

It was a suspicious scene, and Hayward now acted on instinct and drove up to the vehicle.

But, as he did that, the driver pulled the VW out and attempted to flee.

Here's what Hayward wrote in his police report that day:

I was coming off shift and was sitting in my patrol car in front of my house on Hogan Street in Granger. I noticed a gray VW pass me slowly, going south, with its lights off. I checked the license plate but did not recognize that car. After about ten minutes, the sheriff called for some assistance. As I was going up Brock Street, a VW took off, going north at a high rate of speed. I pursued him, also at a high rate of speed. I had the red light on him when he ran the stop sign, but he just went as fast as a Volkswagen would go. I pulled up on him fast, and he finally pulled over into a gas station. He produced his driver's license which identified him as Theodore Robert Bundy, 565 1st Ave, Salt Lake City. The man was wearing dark pants, a black turtleneck with long sleeves, and sneakers. He said he was lost in the subdivision, but he had been there for ten minutes, only a block away from me on Brock Street.

When Hayward apprehended Bundy, having to hold him at gunpoint in the pale light of the empty station, he had no clue he was staring into the eyes of a cold-blooded serial killer or that he was looking at the man who was responsible for so much fear and heartache in this part of the world.

Almost a year had passed since the remains of Janice Ott, Denise Naslund and another young woman had been found near Issaquah, and almost six months had passed since the remains of four other young women had been found at Taylor Mountain, but in this particular moment, all Hayward had was a suspicious feeling that there was something not right about this guy.

This scenario was playing out in real time against a backdrop of stats that had taken months to compile. Those working tirelessly behind the scenes in Washington State had managed to hone in on the name "Ted" after the Lake Sammamish abductions. With that information, they had trawled through records of driver's licences and criminal records, and had tried to build basic databases that they could cross-check with owners of light brown VW Beetles. It sounds easier than it was. At the time, the reality was that the list of light brown VW Beetle owners numbered around 42,000 individuals.

But all of that was in a state far away, and at this point, data was not being shared across state lines and Hayward would have known nothing about Ted Bundy.

Hayward now followed protocol and asked the unruly driver why he was fleeing and driving inconsistently as he did that night.

"I've just been to see a movie," said Bundy without flinching, but Hayward wasn't buying it.

Hayward knew to dig a little deeper and asked Bundy what he had seen.

"Towering Inferno," said Bundy quickly.

It wasn't a bad guess – the film, which starred then-heart-throbs Steve McQueen and Paul Newman, had been released late the previous year and been a critical and commercial success, hailed as one of the best "disaster films" ever. No doubt Bundy had picked up on the zeitgeist and threw the name out in the hope the state trooper would think it made perfect sense. He said he had watched it at the Valley Vu drive-in theatre.

There was just one problem: it wasn't showing anywhere in town.

Hayward had called for a patrol car, and they'd sent a deputy who also witnessed this moment when Bundy suddenly changed his story from "I was at the movies" to "I am lost".

This moment marked a turning point in the macabre life of Ted Bundy.

During the earlier part of their interaction that began just minutes before, Bundy had reverted to his usual "trick" of mixing confidence with fake vulnerability. He stayed calm as he told Hayward he was lost and needed help with directions.

He had stepped out of the car with a big smile plastered on his face and his hands raised. He then conjured up some small talk and threw in the fact that he was studying law at the university, presumably in the hope that this would encourage the state trooper to see him in a different light.

But when it dawned on Bundy that his manufactured stories about being at the movies and then being lost were falling apart, he began to panic. Hayward noted the clear distress and rising anxiety level in the man he had just apprehended.

And things were about to get a whole lot worse for the serial killer.

Hayward did what any official would do: he asked to search the car.

And in that moment, he uncovered the first truly damning evidence against a man who, up until then and despite secret phone calls from his girlfriend to the police, was just another Ted in just another VW Beetle.

The first incriminating evidence was the modification to the vehicle. As Hayward shone his light into the interior of the car, he noticed that the passenger's seat had been removed. He may not have known that Bundy made this change so that his victims could lie flat out of public sight, but he certainly knew it was suspicious.

And there the seat lay on its side on the back seat.

Then, as he searched the car further, he came across other highly incriminating evidence. This included a set of handcuffs, which immediately suggested potential criminal intent in the form of abductions or kidnapping. He also found a variety of burglary tools, including a crowbar and ice pick and, just as alarmingly, a knitted ski mask and pantyhose with holes cut out for eyes – presumably both intended to conceal one's identity during an act of violence.

The New York Times of 10 December 1978 described what happened next: "The suspect changed his story. He had really been smoking marijuana in his car, was befuddled and panicked when a strange car suddenly pulled up behind him, and he sped away to ditch the incriminating evidence. The ski mask and nylon stocking were used for skiing, of course. One of the reasons he chose to study in Utah was the great ski areas, and the river-rafting available on the other side of the massive Wasatch Range. And the handcuffs? Easy – he was a security officer at the university."

Hayward listened to Bundy's stories but he wasn't buying it. Those findings prompted Hayward to arrest Bundy for evading the police and being in possession of burglary tools.

Finally, the brutal serial killer who had cut short the lives of so many young women was in the grip of the authorities, but the full extent of how this man arrested for burglary would prove to be more than a burglar still had to be proven by the law.

In the days that followed, as Bundy's cool facade fell away, he now expressed concern about what the police might know about him and even blurted out that he wanted to call his friend Ann Rule to find out if she knew anything.

Tiffany Jean, who is an archivist, legal librarian and researcher, created a very thorough repository of many documents, photographs and true accounts of Ted Bundy, and in this online repository entitled *Killer in the Archives*, she shares information that shows how Bundy still attempted to keep up his facade of innocence to those who knew him, even as he had his first taste of feeling the might of the law.

Jean's research reveals that, despite the escalating troubles he faced, Bundy minimized the significance of his arrest when recounting it to his downstairs neighbour and occasional girlfriend, Margith Maughan. He claimed he had been out for a drive intending to go to Heber but realized he lacked the funds, leading him to aimlessly cruise around the valley until he ended up in Granger. Maughan recalled that Bundy mentioned noticing a vehicle rapidly approaching from behind, prompting him to accelerate; however, when the police lights activated, he pulled over. He described how officers searched his ashtray for marijuana seeds but found nothing. The patrolman informed him that he was driving the same vehicle that had previously evaded capture, resulting in his arrest. Maughan remembered Bundy stating that he allowed the search of his car. As a law judge's daughter, she questioned his decision, pointing out that they would need a search warrant. Bundy insisted he had nothing to hide and expressed confidence that the officers would not discover anything incriminating.

Meanwhile, in Seattle, his girlfriend Liz Kloepfer was more worried than ever about what Ted was up to. In late September, he called to inform her of his plans to return for a visit. Already suspicious of his possible involvement in the murders, Kloepfer contacted King County Police for advice. They suggested she confront him about the investigation. Kloepfer later recounted that she directly told him she knew about his arrest, to which Bundy responded dismissively, downplaying the situation as merely being stopped for speeding. He claimed it was inconsequential and attributed the police's actions to harassment, asserting that he was simply out driving when they searched his car and labelled it suspicious.

When pressed about why he had fled from the police, Bundy denied running away and attributed any perceived evasion to the officer's agitation. He described the items found in his car as mere junk accumulation and attempted to justify their presence by explaining that a rope from a raft and a crowbar were harmless tools. He further dismissed concerns about pantyhose found in his vehicle by claiming they were used for warmth while shovelling snow. Bundy expressed frustration over the situation and indicated plans to speak with acquaintances to demand they leave him alone.

Kloepfer noted his agitation, and her concern for him grew as he mentioned contacting Ann Rule, a former colleague at the Crisis Clinic who had connections with law enforcement, believing she could provide insight into how much information they possessed about him.

From the perspective of law enforcement, the arrest was significant not only for its immediate implications in the DaRonch case, but also because it was the first time Bundy could possibly be connected to previous crimes.

To Bundy, crossing paths with Hayward was a "freak occurrence", according to the recorded interviews.

At the time that Bob Hayward arrested Bundy, the Salt Lake County Sheriff who he reported to was his own brother, Pete Hayward. Shortly after this strange encounter at 3am, Bob recounted the story to his brother, explaining the unusual nature of the goods found in the car, the seat that had been removed, the articulate and charming law student who had changed his story and the fact that he had seemed to switch from smarmy to shaken in a single second.

In a twist that seems strange all these decades later, Bundy was actually released on bail, but all that was about to change.

When the officials held their next weekly meeting at the sheriff's office, a deputy named Ben Forbes noted that the name of Bob's arrestee was one he had heard before: Theodore Bundy. He said that he had received a photograph from Washington State, where the police had sent it on with a notation saying this man was a potential suspect in the ongoing investigations into the many young women who had disappeared and then been found murdered in that state.

Now the penny was dropping fast. Added to the dots already joined was the composite sketch that had resulted from the abductions of Denise Naslund and Janice Ott at Lake Sammamish, as well as the description of a tan VW Beetle.

Now another detective weighed in. He said there was a seemingly striking connection between the more local Carol DaRonch saga and the paraphernalia found in the car, most notably the handcuffs.

Following these leads, on 21 August, Bundy was taken back into custody by the Utah police for possessing burglary tools, which led to his extended bout of incarceration. Detective Forbes interviewed Bundy, who was notably cooperative, and sought an explanation for the unusual items found in his vehicle.

In his report, Forbes details here how the law student was so skilled at weaving stories to explain away what was found in his vehicle:

Bundy claimed he'd found the handcuffs in a garbage dump in Salt Lake. He informed me that when he was in Seattle he had detained a subject who was stealing a ten-speed bicycle and that he had to scuffle with the party until the police arrived and had no way of restraining him; when he found the handcuffs in this dump up by his apartment, he thought that they would be a good item to carry around in case a similar situation ever arose.

His explanation for the pantyhose with mouth and eye holes cut out and the ski mask was that last winter he had a lot of night classes at the University of Utah and the weather was very cold and he was not used to that. He explained that he was attending late night classes and that he had watched a program on mountaineering, and the climbers used pantyhose masks under their ski masks to stay warm, so he did the same when attending his late night classes.

His explanation for the pieces of white sheet material and rope was that he owns a small raft which he rows around and he used these to tie the oars together and keep everything in a neat bundle.

His explanation for the icepick was that it's a common household piece of equipment.

Bundy was very forthcoming during the interview and "repeated several times that he just wanted to cooperate", according to Forbes, who wasn't fooled by his smart-alec answers.

Added to the mounting evidence against him were Liz's secret phone calls to the police, which were now seen in a different light, and most chilling of all, the authorities finally took cognisance of her description of medical equipment being found in his home. It was all adding up: this evidence now aligned with reports of him feigning injuries to lure his victims.

In short, the police were finally joining the first few dots between all the missing women, the DaRonch case, the Lake Sammamish sightings of the man with his arm in a sling, and the bodies found in Issaquah and on Taylor Mountain.

But it would still take some time.

They first needed DaRonch to strengthen their suspected link between the man who had tried to kidnap her and all the other serious and brutal crimes that had been happening for more than a year.

It was almost a year later, when DaRonch had accepted that the police had not found her attacker and, in fact, had not even found a suspect. She would later describe in *Conversations with a Killer* how it had played on her mind all the time.

"I thought, 'Why can't they find this man?'"

Her house was constantly being watched, and her dad slept with a deer hunting rifle under his bed.

"I tried to move on with my life, but it was always at the back of my mind. 'Where is this guy. Why can't they catch him?'"

Then finally, the tide was about to turn.

She was at home when she received a call from the police station almost a year after she'd survived the attack. They asked her to make her way down to the station to make an identification, and she obliged without hesitation.

For their part, the police had followed protocol, making sure they were not leading the witness in any way. Bundy, for his part, had attempted to throw her off. With a different hairstyle, and clothing very different to the style he wore during her abduction, he stood deadpan in the line-up. As per the law, the officers were present when DaRonch pointed him out.

But though identifying him from the line-up of seven was a cinch for DaRonch, what was much harder was having to stare into the eyes of a man who had wanted nothing more than to kill her on the day he cooked up the plan to abduct her from the mall. She knew those eyes, that jawline, that look …

Ultimately, DaRonch's determination to stand up to her attacker a year before, and now positively identify him, was crucial in bringing him down. Other victims had been silenced by murder, allowing the serial killer to carry on quenching his thirst for harming others.

But this moment of a survivor's bravery at the police station significantly contributed to his arrest and subsequent conviction for aggravated kidnapping in 1976.

This should have been the end of the road for such a menace to society.

Instead, it would be merely the beginning of a hiatus.

13

Facing the Law

Bundy had promised himself no more mistakes after the fiasco at Lake Sammamish. But he had not taken into account the fierce will to live that drove Carol DaRonch to fight back against someone much bigger and stronger and somehow find a way to get away from him, despite the fact that he was armed with a gun and had a pair of handcuffs to use against her.

That attack had occurred in November 1974. He was only arrested nine months later on unrelated charges, but it didn't take long for the police to figure out they had the man they had been searching for in the DaRonch kidnapping. Finally, in February 1976, Ted Bundy appeared in court for the first time to answer for his behaviour. Even though the police had managed to find the key to those handcuffs on the ground in the parking lot where Debra Kent had disappeared that same evening, that was not the case he was going to be answering for. There was still not enough evidence in that case. But Carol DaRonch was a living, breathing eyewitness who was willing to stand up and testify against him.

In later court cases, Bundy chose to represent himself, but this time in court he handed himself over to a defence team that included attorney Bruce Lubeck, an ambitious young lawyer who was not afraid to be aggressive in court. DaRonch would have to use all that courage she had displayed when she was alone with Ted Bundy in his car to get through the trial.

She didn't waver once. She was able to positively identify him in the courtroom as her attacker, and when she was put on the stand, she stuck to her story, despite Bruce Lubeck's forceful cross-examination. Lubeck believed that far too much time had elapsed between the incident and the police line-up for Carol DaRonch to be able to credibly identify his client. Lubeck also called a psychologist who was an expert in "eyewitness testimony" to the stand as a witness. That expert explained how traumatic events – particularly those involving violence or extreme stress – can distort a witness's recall. Even more damaging to the prosecution's case was the expert's assertion that identifications made months or years after an incident were inherently unreliable. Time, the expert testified, did not merely fade memories; it actively reshaped them, making witnesses unconsciously more confident in details that might be entirely false.

"I remember being on the witness stand for hours," DaRonch said. "Being questioned by his attorneys, trying to say that I didn't have the right man, of course, and how did I know that he was the right man. That I was mistaken."

But DaRonch knew she had her man, and nothing could make her change her mind.

Aside from the questions being asked about her truthfulness, the thing that DaRonch remembers most clearly from the trial was the look on Ted Bundy's face when the participants were discussing what had happened. "He was down there sitting with a smirk on his face, always really arrogant, kind of laughing when I'd answer the questions," she said.

A key witness in trial was the woman whose car Carol had jumped into, a woman named Mary Walsh. She brought a new perspective to the courtroom, describing in minute detail the terror that Carol endured.

She said it was misty on the evening of the attack, and she looked out of the window at a school to her left, and when she turned her head back again, "This young girl was right in front of us, just popped out of the mist, and she was right in front of our headlights. And we slammed on the brakes."

She said that because it was dark and misty, she and her husband got quite a large fright when Carol appeared in the headlights.

At first, they were confused and quickly locked the doors as they wondered why this stranger was trying to stop their car, but when they saw how terrified she was, they realized she was trying to jump into the car for help, not to harm them.

"I have never seen a human being that frightened in my life. She was trembling and crying, and almost weak, like she was going to faint, and she was just in a terrible state," she recalled.

Then Mary spotted the handcuffs and became even more confused.

She said in court that when you see someone in cuffs, your immediate assumption is that they're escaping from something or someone related to the police force.

But the terrified Carol was mumbling and in her shocked state kept saying, "I can't believe it, I can't believe it."

Mary then put her arm around Carol and tried to calm her so they could figure out what was wrong and what had happened. But Carol was still in such shock that it was difficult to get her to calm down enough to be coherent. She just kept saying, "He was going to kill me, he was going to kill me if I didn't stop screaming."

Mary described how Carol wanted to go straight to the police station, and still in her state of shock, began to talk about the gun.

"She was upset and trembling so badly that as we were driving to the police station, we calmed her down a little bit because I was holding her so tight. She then said that he had a gun to her head. And I remember thinking, what a terrible experience, and that's why she was so frightened. Then I asked her, well, what had happened, and she had said something about him taking her out of the fashion mall. And I thought it was kind of a strange thing because of so many people, if he dragged her out. Then she said he pretended he was a security guard for the mall."

Mary said that Carol managed to say that the attacker was in a battered-up VW and that he'd tried to use a crowbar to hit her.

Mary also saw that Carol's shoe was missing, and that as she got of out the car, she went limp and nearly fainted.

The testimonies were strong, and the trial was relatively brief and had wrapped up by early March. Ted Bundy was found guilty of kidnapping and received an indeterminate sentence of one to fifteen years. That means that the minimum of one year represents the absolute shortest time an inmate must serve, while fifteen years marks the outer limit of their incarceration. What happens between those two points depends entirely on the prisoner's behaviour, rehabilitation efforts and the judgement of the parole board.

Many people were surprised, and a little offended, that the sentence was so light and that he could conceivably be out in a few years' time. People also knew how Bundy was the prime suspect in many other murders and wanted him charged for those, but Captain Pete Hayward insisted that there was no physical evidence to link Bundy with those crimes, although there was inferential evidence.

Even after the sentencing, attorney Bruce Lubeck maintained that Bundy had been wrongfully accused, telling a television interviewer, "We have our theories as to how it happened and why she did make an identification, but I don't conclude that it was because she got a good look at her abductor and was able to remember him. I don't think that happened."

What Bundy did know as he began his sentence was that in November of 1975, a group of thirty investigators had spent some time gathered at a Holiday Inn in Aspen, Colorado, to discuss the peculiar case of Ted Bundy. *The New York Times* reported: "In addition to the brutal sex slayings in Washington and Utah, the suspect was now being linked to the Colorado deaths. A check of his Chevron gasoline credit card showed him buying gas on the same days and in the same communities where three young women had vanished – two of whom have never been seen since. Taking these cases, plus the murders of two other young Colorado women, the police compared the facts with the Utah and Washington slayings and came up with what the group in the motel believed was a convincing track of one killer."

Each recovered body told the same brutal story: a young woman found naked, her skull savagely crushed from behind. Those discovered before nature had taken its toll revealed evidence of sexual assault and mutilation. The victims formed a chilling pattern – all attractive young women in their teens or twenties, all slim with long brown hair parted in the middle, all wearing pierced earrings.

"The evidence was slim, little of it could be introduced as evidence into a court of law, but the lawmen left the meeting convinced they had their man."

Knowing that Bundy was already languishing in prison, the investigators took their time preparing a case. They applied their focus to the murder of Caryn Campbell after they found an eyewitness who could place Bundy in the ski lodge on the night of the murder. Plus they had his gas slips, which placed

Bundy in Aspen on the day of the murder, and the microscopic hair evidence from the car. The evidence was presented to a grand jury, who concluded that there was enough with which to charge Bundy for murder.

When he was told in October 1977 that a charge of murder had been laid in the case of Caryn Campbell, Bundy told a reporter, "There are a lot of police egos on the line. The issue a long time ago was whether I was innocent or guilty. The issue is now: 'Can we pin it on him?'"

In January of 1977, having served nearly a year of his kidnapping sentence, Ted Bundy was extradited to Colorado to prepare for the upcoming murder trial. This time, he wanted to play a much bigger role in his own defence. And one of the witnesses who would be called to testify against him? None other than Carol DaRonch.

14

Two Brazen Escapes from Justice

Bundy had thought about little else but getting out ever since he was locked away for the kidnapping of Carol DaRonch. From the moment he first set foot in the Pitkin County Courthouse in Aspen, Colorado, he realized this would be the best opportunity he was going to get. Built in 1890, the historic old Victorian structure, with its large, arched windows, red brick facade and shallow roof with a large prominent spire, is set back from the street and surrounded by large, attractive trees and thick shrubbery, giving it an air of calm authority.

Standing above the entrance is the familiar statue of Lady Justice holding weighted scales in her hands as she presides over the fate of the many citizens, innocent and guilty, who pass through the wooden doors to hear judgement being passed on their actions. But in this courthouse, unlike in most American justice facilities, the Lady is not blindfolded. She has been sculpted with her eyes wide open. The courthouse was elegant and functioned well, but it was a far cry from a heavily secured facility.

Bundy was clearly a criminal genius. He was able to create elaborate plans and schemes that would confound law enforcement for years. He used deception, false names, stories and disguises that led him to fool young women into trusting him over and over again. But when it came to his escape, he kept it as simple as possible. In all honesty, he didn't need much of a plan. He had elected to represent himself alongside some qualified lawyers. In his always overconfident way, he imagined he was finally putting his years of legal training to good use, even though he never actually completed his degree. But to the court, his status as an "attorney" in an active case gave him the kind of freedom of movement that would have been impossible if he had just been a defendant in a criminal case. During the pre-trial period, Bundy was allowed to move around the courthouse without handcuffs or leg shackles impeding his movement, and he was given access to the law library to do research on his defence.

On 7 June 1977, Bundy appeared in court for the day's proceedings wearing tan corduroy slacks and a beige turtleneck shirt with a tan sweater over it. During a mid-morning court recess, he asked to be escorted up to the law library on the second floor of the courthouse. He was accompanied by a single guard, who escorted him up to the library, watched him go inside, and then stationed himself in the passage and waited for Bundy to complete the research he was doing for the case. Bundy walked deep into the room and started wandering between the tall, overloaded bookshelves that provided such good cover. He made sure there was no one else present, keeping his eye on the door, then walked around until he found a position that was shielded from the guard's vision.

Behind him, the tall wooden window frames were open. He looked outside to see if there was anyone there, but it was all quiet. "The fresh air was blowing through, and the sky was blue, and I said, 'I'm ready to go,' and I walked to the window and jumped out."

From the second-story library window to the ground below was a 25-foot drop onto grass. It was a risky jump but not impossible, and when the moment came, Bundy barely hesitated. It all happened so quickly that nobody inside the courthouse suspected a thing.

He landed hard on his ankle, but not so badly that he couldn't move. Since he had come up with the idea in the cell where he was being held, Ted had been practising jumping from the top bunk of his cell in an effort to strengthen his ankles and learn how to minimize the impact of the fall. He had also been figuring out the distance to the riverbed that ran across the edge of town and the mountains beyond Aspen where he would need to get to if he was to have any reasonable chance of not being caught. He had been running that distance inside his cell over and over again and was in pretty good shape by the time he did. Outside the court, Bundy looked around, saw that he was in the clear and hobbled away on his swollen ankle as quickly as he could, crossing the Roaring Fork River and heading for the trailhead that signalled the start of the thickly wooded area.

Only a couple of miles northeast of the courthouse, the imposing vista of Smuggler Mountain and the White River National Forest were beckoning to him. This wild and untamed natural area full of hiking trails and summer cabins would be the perfect refuge from the authorities. Ted thought of himself as adept in the mountains, as he had often found himself far out and alone in the wild as he disposed of his victims.

Back inside the courthouse, the guard still manning the door was sitting quietly and waiting when he heard a commotion from the bottom of the stairs. He listened hard and heard something about a man jumping out of a window. With a sinking feeling, the guard burst into the library and started looking around frantically, shouting, "Bundy! Bundy!" and running up and down the rows of books until he turned a corner and came face to face with the wide-open window frames that looked past Lady Justice and out towards the wilderness. He looked out in disbelief, almost hoping that he would see Ted Bundy still lying there on the grass, but there was nothing but a deep indentation in the earth where his prisoner had landed with a thump. With the blood pounding in his ears, the guard turned around and rushed down to the street to see if anyone had seen the defendant.

Outside the courthouse, the police and security guards spread out to comb the area for the escaped murderer. Inside the courtroom, officials noticed that the sweater he had been wearing earlier that morning was still there, and they began to realize that he had appeared bulging and uncomfortable that morning, almost as if there had been another garment he had been wearing underneath the shirt. That meant he was out there in a change of clothes and they would not be able to provide a description of what he was wearing.

The local authorities went into full crisis mode. Heads would roll over this incident, but the number one priority was to recapture one of the most infamous prisoners in the United States, who had escaped on their watch.

Moving cautiously through the sleepy resort town, Bundy began to pick up his pace. He was simply incredulous that his brazen plan had worked so well. Reaching the mountains, he climbed hard off the beaten paths for an hour or so until finally he turned to look back at the quiet town of Aspen, which lay far below him. Up here, the chances of running into someone from law enforcement were extremely narrow. When the wind swirled, he could occasionally hear the sound of police sirens driving around town. That let him know that his escape had been detected and that he was now officially a fugitive from justice. He expected there would be planes and helicopters flying overhead shortly.

He realized he needed to find shelter and a place to rest while he figured out where to go and what to do. Just before it started to rain, Bundy stumbled upon a secluded wooden cabin about seven miles from the centre of town that seemed well cared for but was currently uninhabited. He approached warily, looking for any signs of life or movement, but when he was convinced that it was empty, he broke in and was finally able to sit down comfortably and take the weight off his swollen ankle.

That night, Bundy ate what he could find in the cabin and then lay low for the next few days, while newspaper and television headlines exploded with the news of his daring escape. "Slay suspect escapes in leap from window," proclaimed the headline in *Rocky Mountain News* the following day. In the article, the writer followed up with this mesmerizing detail about the escape: "Ms. Marcia De Camp, a secretary in the sheriff's office, said nobody realized Bundy had escaped until an unidentified passerby ran up to her in the basement of the courthouse about 10:45 am and inquired: 'Is it normal for people to jump out of second story windows around here?'"

One local, a woman named Jan Robinson, told *The Denver Post* – which ran a column on the front page saying "Aspen starts door-to-door Bundy search" – that the incident "reminds me of a slapstick comedy where everything goes wrong".

A manhunt was launched that involved over 150 residents and law enforcement officials pulled in from the neighbouring towns. Within the first few hours, roadblocks were set up on both sides of town, and all vehicles leaving via the Colorado 82 were pulled over and searched in case they were, knowingly or unknowingly, harbouring the fugitive.

Reports of sightings began to come in and were followed up as quickly as possible. Someone claimed they had seen him approaching a condominium complex on the east of town; other sightings seemed to confirm that he had been moving to the east. As they waited for a break in the case, the law enforcement officials made a reasonable assumption that Bundy would be heading for the thickly wooded hills. A surveillance helicopter from neighbouring Grand Junction was pulled into action, while a team of six search dogs started combing the mountains looking to pick up his scent.

But despite Ted Bundy's fearsome reputation and the real possibility that there was a killer on the loose in their neighbourhood, many residents of the laid-back town met the news with a shrug. They didn't seem to be fearing for their safety. Reporters Joseph Seldner and Pam Parker penned a story titled "Bundy Escape Miffs 'Unfrightened' Aspen". The two reporters found that the "bars were at least as full as normal and single women were walking around". Mayor Stacy Standley said that most people were not scared but they were "miffed" that this had happened. The vast majority thought they were in no danger because they tried to put themselves in his shoes, and believed there was simply no way that a fugitive would hang around in Aspen. That was the last place they would be, with all this nature out there. They believed he was probably already miles away in the vast, empty mountain ranges that surrounded the resort town. In the same article, city manager Philip Mahoney agreed that most residents were not at all scared and that the one who should be worried, if he was out there alone in the mountains, was Bundy himself. "It's rugged country up there," he said. "Bundy is probably a scared man right now."

Nobody knows whether Bundy was scared or not, but he was in a difficult situation, and he was smart enough to know that he had to do something or he would get caught. He had no food, no transport, no money and only the clothes on his back. A surprising cold snap in the weather made things even more difficult for him, and after almost a week with nothing to eat, his strength began to fade quickly.

Finally, he had to move, so he abandoned the cabin and headed south toward Crested Butte. What would have been a straightforward journey for an ordinary hiker was a desperate ordeal for a fugitive. For the next 48 hours, he stumbled through the Colorado wilderness, missing not one but two trails that could have led him to safety. He was lost, hungry and his foot needed some medical attention and a lot of recuperation.

On June 10, desperation drove him to break into a camping trailer at Maroon Lake, approximately ten miles from Aspen. He took only what he needed to survive: food and a ski parka, but there was nothing that could really change his fortunes there – like a car. Instead of continuing south, Bundy made a mistake and turned back north toward Aspen and people.

Three nights later, on 13 June, Bundy was all out of options. He had to go into town, so he crept along by the light of the moon until he found himself alongside a quiet golf course. In the parking area, he saw cars that looked like a fairly easy target. He started going from one parked car to another until he found what he was looking for – an unlocked Volkswagen with the keys still inside. He slid the door open, sat down heavily, then started it up and hit the road.

But it was only a week since he had gone missing, and the authorities were still on high alert and they got lucky. Sometime after midnight, Pitkin County officers Maureen Higgins and Gene Flatt were out on a routine investigation when they saw a car make an unusual U-turn while driving. Flatt told TV reporters later that they "noted a vehicle that was driving erratically about a eighth of a mile east of Aspen on Highway 82". Once they observed the vehicle, Flatt turned his patrol car around and set off in pursuit of the car. Once they spotted it, they pulled up alongside the Volkswagen and gestured to the driver to pull over, which he did. Asked whether he recognized Bundy right away, Flatt admits that it "took about two glances.

His appearance had been altered by glasses and a minor growth of beard." But it was him. Bundy was exhausted and had no fight left in him. When the officer asked for his driver's licence, he pretended to scratch around and look for it while making up a lame story about leaving the valley for good. He offered no resistance when they pulled him out of the car and handcuffed him.

Back in the county jail, TV news reported that "he had lost about fifteen pounds. His body was scratched. He injured his knee while mountain climbing. He was exhausted and disoriented."

But no permanent damage had been done and Bundy was soon back to himself. Bundy grinned when asked what he had done, as if it had just been playing a game of hide-and-seek. He told anyone who would listen about his adventurous week out in the woods.

On the *Conversations with a Killer* documentary, someone asks him why he had attempted an escape, and he admitted that "I just got sick and tired of being locked up. I had – over a number of months – I had noticed a number of opportunities to just walk right out." He even tried to put a positive spin on what had happened, spinning it as an example of the traditional American yearning for freedom and adventure. "I just longed for freedom for so long and now I'm like … I was living my ultimate dream. It was an incredible experience."

He went on to relate how close the authorities had been to finding him a few times. They had even searched the cabin where he had been hiding one day, but luckily for him, he was out in the woods when that happened. That night he slept out in the open in case the cops had found something and decided to come back and get him. On another occasion, the search helicopter had landed only a hundred feet away from him, but again, they had failed to spot him.

Back before the judge, this time with shackles around his ankles and handcuffs on, he was informed that he would be facing additional charges of escape, second-degree burglary, misdemeanour theft and a felony theft, which carried a possible ninety years imprisonment.

Yet Bundy seemed almost relieved about being back in civilization, despite being a prisoner again. Clearly, he had many talents, but being an outdoorsman was not one of them. He told officers that he was glad it was over.

It was over the next few weeks that his correspondence with Carole Ann Boone became deeper and more intimate. He told her about his life in jail and was able to make her believe that all of this was just ridiculous and a travesty of justice for him to have been arrested. She believed it hook, line and sinker. She even came to visit him in prison in Utah and was taken aback at how much his appearance had changed. "I was shocked," she said later, "to see him in a cell, to see that loss of movement, of freedom. It is hard to describe except that in some strange way, he was as far away, as far removed, as a person can be."

Determined not to let him escape again, the authorities transferred Ted to the Garfield County Jail in Glenwood Springs, Colorado, and severely curtailed his ability to move around the courthouse unimpeded, despite the fact that he was still legally representing himself. When the trial got underway and he was formally facing the charge of murdering Caryn Campbell, all the usual good fortune that had deserted Ted Bundy when he was alone in the mountains seemed to be back in effect. A series of pretrial motions had gone in his favour, then a number of pieces of evidence were ruled as inadmissible, and the whole case against him started to seem like it was built on flimsy foundations.

There was a sense building that he would beat these charges and that he would only have to serve time for the aggravated kidnapping of Carol DaRonch. Life wasn't too bad. He was receiving thoughtful care packages from Carole Ann Boone that included many choice prison items, such as parcels filled with protein powder, dried fruit, vitamins, cash and even niceties like cologne. Stephen Michaud noted, "A more rational defendant might have realized that he stood a good chance of acquittal, and that beating the murder charge in Colorado would probably have dissuaded other prosecutors to try and pin him down ... with as little as a year and a half to serve on the DaRonch conviction, had Ted persevered [with the Campbell trial], he could have been a free man."

But once again, Bundy could not just sit quietly and let things unfold. He saw an opportunity to get away and, in his calm, systematic way, he began to work towards it. First, he was able to obtain a detailed floor plan of the jail from one of the other inmates. This gave him the ability to map out his potential route to freedom. Next, he bought a small hacksaw that was strong enough to saw through metal. Next, he addressed the issue of finances. One of the biggest problems after his first escape was a lack of cash, and he didn't want to make that mistake again.

Through various supporters, including his girlfriend Carole Ann Boone, he was able to stash away nearly $500 in cash – the equivalent of over $2,000 in today's terms – which would give him a fair number of options if he ever got back into the outside world again. By now, there was no disguising the relationship between Carole and Ted. Her letters from that period make it crystal clear that her faith in him and his innocence was total. "I've come to such a caring and commitment to you ... I want to be close enough to at least make phone calls, and visit ... be there if I can help. And be in the same part of the world as you, for me. It's hard to explain, but I need you … the affection that I get, and that which I feel. I've been around enough to know that such affection, such caring is a blessed, treasurable thing … dearest Bunny … I know you are innocent, and I know there's a way for you to be free …"

Bundy had figured out that the best escape route open to him was through the roof of his prison cell. He had realized there was a lighting fixture that was mounted in the ceiling that could be pushed out into a crawl space above the cell. So every night, during the prison shower routine, when other prisoners were distracted or in the bathroom, he would work meticulously to make the opening in the roof slightly bigger by sawing through the thick ceiling panels to create a hole roughly one square foot in size. The only problem was that the air ducts above the ceiling were too small for a man of his size to get through, but Bundy wasn't defeated by that.

He began to starve himself over the next few months until he had lost around 35 pounds, and he was able to wriggle his way up into the crawl space above his cell. According to Undersheriff Robert A. Hart, the prisoner had weighed 170 pounds when he was first placed into custody, but by the time he escaped, he weighed no more than 140 pounds. None of his jailers ever thought to question why he was losing so much weight. They couldn't imagine anyone doing such meticulous forward-planning or being that committed to getting out.

While he may have been able to hide the fact that he was sawing a hole in the ceiling, there was no disguising the sounds of someone moving around inside the roof above the cellblock at night.

There were multiple reports from an informant of suspicious night-time movement above the ceiling, but Bundy's luck held once again, and these reports went completely uninvestigated by the guards. For weeks, Bundy covertly explored the network of confined spaces in the jailhouse and plotted his next move. It seems that somehow Carole Ann became aware of what he was planning to do and wrote him a letter which read, "I understand the solutions you see to your problems, especially the (your) preferred one. But I keep feeling … so very strongly that there is something else. Another way … An extremely unfortunate set of events and people have put you, most unjustly, into your cell in Garfield County, Colorado. There is a way (one at least) to get you back out of that maze. Finding it, making it happen, hasn't taken place. Yet. But I am dead certain it is there. And am dead certain that it will happen."

In the weeks leading up to the trial, the case had become something of a *cause célèbre* in Aspen. The severity of the charges against him, the fact that Bundy was such an unlikely-looking criminal and the audacity of his jump out of the window brought him lots of attention. Bundy decided to use that to his advantage, by claiming that he could no longer get a fair trial in Aspen. He filed a motion to change the venue of his upcoming trial to Denver, where he imagined he would be judged less severely, or at least buy himself some time. The judge granted his request to move the trial from Aspen, but instead of Denver, he decided it would go ahead in Colorado Springs, a small town that was not only the home town of El Paso County District Attorney Robert Russel, but also had a reputation for dealing quite harshly with murder suspects like Ted Bundy.

Bundy was stunned to not be going to Denver and was not about to accept this news graciously or without making his opinion felt. Inside the courtroom, he raised a finger threateningly, pointed it at the judge and hissed at him, "You are sentencing me to death!" Bundy realized that the trial must not go ahead in Colorado Springs. It was time to make his move. He judged correctly that the New Year's weekend would be when the guards were at their most distracted and the system at its most vulnerable.

So on 30 December 1977, he sprung into action, placing a set of his books and clothes under the blankets to make it look like he was sleeping, then he built up another pile of books that he could climb up to reach the hole in the ceiling and escape out of his cell. Once he was in the crawl space, he broke into the apartment of the chief jailer, who was out with his wife enjoying some holiday festivities. Inside the man's apartment, Bundy quickly changed into a pair of his blue jeans, a grey turtleneck sweater and blue sneakers. Then he simply walked out of the front door towards freedom. This time around, he had money, he was not injured, and it would be hours before it was discovered that he was even missing.

The last time anyone had eyes on their most famous inmate was at 7pm on Friday evening when Bundy told Officer Frank Perry that he wasn't feeling well and was going to have an early night. In his report on how Bundy had escaped, Officer Perry provided a detailed portrait of how the night unfolded. He claims to have checked in on the sleeping form of Bundy at midnight, 1.30am and again at 3am. "On 12-31-77 @8am, Delores served breakfast she called Mr. Bundy but no answer, she told me he sometimes didn't eat because he hadn't felt well, I looked in to check and saw him on the bunk (or I assumed it was him) and told Delores to let him sleep."

Later on that day, a letter was received for Bundy and was placed upon his food tray. Still, there was no response from him, and finally, their suspicions were aroused when the letter was still sitting there untouched and the prisoner had not moved at all. Perry writes, "I then went in the cell, everything looked in place, he had the same shirt on that he had the night before when we talked. I went to shake him but felt nothing but paper for his arm, wastebasket for shoulders, books for body and legs,

I thought he was playing a joke on me. I looked in the shower and under his bunk, that is when I thought it was time to call Undersheriff Hart."

By the time it was discovered that the plate of food was untouched and that there was no Bundy in the cell, it was already noon on Saturday, the last day of the year. He had been on the loose for 17 hours before the alarm was raised.

District Attorney Russel, having spent months preparing for the case, was shocked, telling *The Denver Post* that "this just makes me sick. I just don't understand the lack of precaution. I'd think with the history on this man, they'd double-check their facilities."

Twenty minutes after it was discovered that he was gone again, just like six months earlier in the year, roadblocks were once again erected on all the major routes leading out of town. Police protection was also granted to Carol DaRonch, as law enforcement wanted to make sure that Bundy would not be looking to exact retribution on the only woman who had managed to send him behind bars.

But this time around, Bundy would not be making the same mistakes again. He was long gone.

The Colorado police forces were stung by how bad this whole saga made them look. They began frantically phoning around, contacting people like Liz Kloepfer, Ted's mother, his siblings, his co-workers from the Republican Party and anyone else they could think of. On the phone, they would threaten those acquaintances with arrest in a desperate effort to get any kinds of leads or ideas as to where he could possibly be headed.

Three days after he escaped from custody, the FBI was brought in to help the investigation. Special Agent John Reed of the FBI held a press conference and announced that "a federal warrant was issued on January 5, 1978 at Denver, Colorado charging Bundy with unlawful flight to avoid prosecution for the crime of murder."

That was less threatening than it seemed. In the late 1970s, the Federal Bureau of Investigation was far from being the technological powerhouse it would later become. When local law enforcement called in the FBI to hunt Ted Bundy, they discovered an uncomfortable truth: the Bureau's reach was not a lot better than their own.

While television shows portrayed federal agents as omniscient crime fighters, the reality was far more mundane. There were no sprawling digital databases to work with, no instant nationwide alerts, no real-time communication networks that could be mobilized. News of Bundy's crimes and escapes travelled at the speed of newspaper delivery and evening broadcasts, and time and again, during the critical hours and days after an attack, while journalists were still typing up their reports and television stations were processing their film footage, Bundy would be able to cross state lines virtually undetected.

This technological void created a killer's paradise. By the time a young woman's disappearance made the evening news in one state, Bundy could be hundreds of miles away, anonymous in another jurisdiction, planning his next attack. The FBI's much-vaunted involvement in the case amounted to little more than more boots on the ground – agents knocking on doors and showing photographs, just like their local counterparts. In an age before instant communication, even the nation's premier law enforcement agency could not close the gap between a killer's movements and society's awareness of the danger that stalked its streets.

Ted Bundy knew all of the strengths and the weaknesses of crime fighters. He was also self-aware enough to know what he needed to do to remain a free man. He told Stephen Michaud that "the FBI knows that people are essentially creatures of habit. That we have our little habits that we like to perform over and over again. And they just wait for people to assume those habits again."

Ted realized that he needed to change his identity in order to escape the dragnet that was being put up to catch him. "The person has to examine his life and say, 'What parts of my life are distinctive?' and then change them. Creating an identity is not terribly difficult to do at all."

Bundy's meticulous planning and physical transformation allowed him to pull off one of the most daring jailbreaks in American history. As word spread about what he had done, there was outrage and horror among the general public. But a grudging respect was also present. This second escape was a chilling testament to the lengths that this cunning, determined criminal would go to in the pursuit of his own personal freedom.

The first thing that Bundy did once he was a free man was to steal a car and try to get as far away from Glenwood Springs as possible. He headed out of town on Interstate 70, the major east–west highway that runs all the way from Utah to Baltimore, Maryland. But he had been hasty in his selection of a vehicle, and before he had even managed to drive 100 miles, the car came to a grinding halt before he had crossed state lines. Undeterred, Bundy abandoned the car, stuck out his thumb and managed to catch a ride from a passing motorist to the town of Vail, Colorado.

From Vail, it was another 100 miles along I-70 to the sprawling city of Denver, Colorado, where Bundy decided that he would be able to blend into the crowds and evade capture. He hopped on a bus heading for Denver and made it in time to the airport, where he was able to catch a morning flight from Denver to Chicago. By the time the staff realized that he was gone, Ted Bundy was over a thousand miles away in a major metropolis where he would easily be able to blend into the crowds. But Bundy was far from done – he made his way to the train station and bought a ticket to board an Amtrak train that was making a beeline east to the student-heavy town of Ann Arbor on the outskirts of Detroit, Michigan

Somehow, he had found out that his alma mater, the University of Washington, was playing in the Rose Bowl football game against the University of Michigan. Ted knew that the Rose Bowl was the oldest post-season game in American football history, and that it was always a prestigious event that attracted thousands of spectators. Ann Arbor was flooded with excited football fans – exactly the kind of place where he could blend in completely. In town, Ted found a local tavern where he could watch the game and get drunk with a group of his peers and pretend that he was just one of them again. But it didn't go smoothly; he drank a little too much, his support for the visitors from Washington was too vocal and he almost got himself beaten up by a group of Michigan supporters.

That night, he wandered around the college town looking for a place to sleep. Most places were fully booked, and Ted desperately needed some privacy. Eventually, he stumbled upon the Methodist Church, where he was able to sleep rough without being disturbed by anyone.

The next morning, feeling refreshed, he stole a car and drove across state lines heading south. After driving all day down the I-75, he ended up in Atlanta, where he abandoned the car and hopped on a bus heading to the city of Tallahassee in the Sunshine State of Florida, which was almost 2,000 miles away from where he had escaped.

There were a number of reasons for choosing the state of Florida, the chief one being that it was literally as far away from the scenes of his crimes as he could get while staying within the United States. Ted reasoned that no one in Florida would even have heard the name Ted Bundy, let alone be looking for him all that way, and he was right.

Tallahassee was also home to Florida State University (FSU), a campus that was home to thousands of young men and women. It was the kind of place where Ted had found victims easy to come by over and over again. This was the kind of environment he knew well, where he would blend in easily and wait for the furore over his escape to die down. He had good memories of visiting the Sunshine State – this was the state that he had visited in 1968 as part of the Republican National Convention when his life was still very much on track and where he had harboured high hopes of becoming the kind of man that wielded power and influence in modern American life. Perhaps there was some kind of subconscious urge to regain that kind of status and confidence that he had enjoyed during those few days at the apex of American power that led him to Florida.

On a quiet Sunday evening in January 1978, while the Garzaniti family of Tallahassee settled in to watch Burt Reynolds in *Gator* on television, Ted Bundy stood in the darkness staring at their house and sizing up the car that was sitting in their driveway. Rick Garzaniti, his wife, and their young child had no idea that one of America's most wanted fugitives was mere feet away and looking in their living room window as he had done through so many windows for so many years previously. As the opening credits of the movie rolled across their television screen, Bundy was satisfied that they were engrossed enough in what they were watching, and he turned his attention to their orange 1972 Volkswagen Super Beetle – the default getaway car that he'd chosen over and over again to aid him while cutting a swathe of terror across the continental United States.

The robbery proceeded without incident, and once again, Ted Bundy was living as a free man in a college town with a

VW Beetle at his disposal and some cash in his pocket. It had been three years since the murder of Caryn Campbell, and since then, he had been denied the ability to practise what he considered his unique gift. All his talent and energy had been spent trying to escape from the long arm of the law. Now that he was on his own again, the hunger to kill returned with a ferocity that surprised even Bundy. He knew that he would not be satisfied by anything other than being alone in a room with a terrified young woman and a weapon with which to bludgeon her to death.

It was only a matter of time before some poor, unlucky young student would find herself firmly in his sights.

15

Murder in the Sorority

Of all the brutal murders that Ted Bundy committed in the 1970s, perhaps the most preventable and therefore tragic were those that took place after he had escaped to Florida. Firstly, in the early hours of the morning on 15 January in 1978, were the Chi Omega murders. Unlike his earlier serial killings in the northwest when nobody knew yet who he was, this time around Bundy was a well-known figure who had already escaped twice from the clutches of the authorities, and he should never have been let loose on the unsuspecting public.

One would think that with everything mounting up against him, he'd resist the temptation to do it again knowing that a nationwide manhunt was almost certainly underway to search for an escapee from prison. But one thing was certain: Ted Bundy's thirst for killing was so complete and all-consuming that almost nothing in the world would stop him from trying to quench it.

In Tallahassee that winter, the hapless victims would be a group of young women who were soundly asleep in their sorority house. As the evidence showed, the attack was cold-blooded and carefully planned.

Bundy had arrived in Tallahassee, Florida, on 7 January 1978 after a six-hour bus ride from Atlanta at the tail end of a long journey from the prison that had entailed various forms of transport.

He disembarked from the bus and, a few days thereafter, settled into his room at The Oak, a simple boarding house located close by to Florida State University. The simple two-story dwelling, with its white clapboard facade and vintage calligraphic signage, had always been a convenient choice for students at the university because of its affordability and proximity to the campus.

For Bundy, it had other "conveniences" too. For one, he was able to scout out the area and identify potential victims, with the lodgings being a short walk from campus.

Another advantage he had was that here, he could rely on his old trick of blending in as a "normal" man in an academic milieu, socializing with women at the lodgings and using his powers of articulation to chat, build connections and blend in.

By the time he settled into his chair at Sherrod's, a local bar and disco adjacent to the campus and very close to the Chi Omega sorority house on the night of 14 January, it seems he had carefully planned what would happen under the cloak of darkness within the next few hours.

But while his behaviour might have made other patrons uneasy, it did not arouse enough suspicion for anyone to call security.

Terri Murphy was a member of the Chi Omega sorority and was living at the house. That winter, she had a job at Sherrod's, where she earned a little pocket money for her life as a student. She happened to be on duty on the night of 14 January. The bar, of course, drew many types, but by far those in the majority were young students looking for fun and connection. As can be expected of such a place, there was always a sprinkling of single men who did not appear to be students and were there to try to pick someone up.

Terri noticed quite a few of them in the disco that night, but there were three that stood out. She noticed them standing in a corner towards the south end of the building, right near the bathrooms, at the same end of the bar where she was working. It looked as if two of them knew each other and were there together, chatting and drinking. The third one appeared to be more of a loner and didn't quite seem to fit in. When he asked her to fix him a drink, he was, in her own words, "overly polite".

At around 2.35am, she finished up her shift, pulled on a warm winter jacket and headed off on foot to the sorority house. She would not think of that strange man again until later, when the law would request her to do so.

That same night, earlier in the evening, students Mary Ann Picano and Connie Hastings were also at Sherrod's. They had arrived around 10pm and were up for a fun Saturday night. They noticed a white man "standing alone watching the rest of the people". He had medium brown hair, was in his early thirties, and wore layers of clothing.

Before long, the man asked Mary Ann if she'd like to dance. Despite the fact that he gave her the creeps, she said yes, and as she headed off to the dance floor with him, she turned to her friend and, by way of making fun of the man's clothes, joked, "I think I'm going to dance with an ex-con."

Through the noise of the music, the man tried to make small talk with her. His attempts at charm had the opposite effect on Mary Ann, who, instead, couldn't shake the feeling that something was off with him.

He tried to make eye contact with her, but she avoided his gaze and felt so "uneasy" after the brief encounter that she and her friends decided to leave the venue altogether.

Another Florida State University student, Carla Black, had also noticed the out-of-place-looking man at Sherrod's. She was a part-time employee in the Registrar's Graduation Department, and this job, coupled with her studies, meant she had had a busy week. It being Saturday night, she realized she needed to unwind a little and took herself off to Sherrod's bar late on the night of 14 January 1978. She arrived with her sorority sister, Valerie, and the pair stayed until the bar closed after 2am.

Like the others that night, as she settled in with a drink, Carla noticed a man who seemed out of place among the typical college crowd. His attire and age set him apart, and his greasy appearance caught her attention. He stood apart in the northwest corner of the bar, near an exit that led directly to the Chi Omega sorority house. For about half an hour, she observed him from a well-lit area near the dance floor, feeling increasingly uneasy as he stared at her.

Initially, Carla thought his gaze might be flirtatious, but as time passed, it became apparent that his demeanour was more unsettling than that. He looked at her and other women with what she would later describe as a "rude" stare, often smirking as if he felt superior or privy to some secret. At one point, she watched him turn his head to stare openly at the buttocks of an attractive girl walking by. This only augmented her discomfort with his behaviour.

Throughout the evening at Sherrod's, Carla spotted this man in three different areas of the bar. When she first entered, he was near the front bar area, but it was only later, when he had taken up residence in the northeast section leaning against a wall, that she saw him unashamedly fixating on her and others.

Carla would later describe him as a white male, likely between 28 and 30 years old with a medium build and greasy hair. He wore high-waisted knit pants and his shoes were black patent leather with pointed toes. These were details she remembered vividly, as she often looked down to avoid his gaze.

Like many others, she got spooked by Bundy on sight and did her best to avoid him, but never in her wildest dreams could she have anticipated what happened next.

All these eyewitness accounts were crucial for piecing together events leading up to the attacks. However, what seemed like odd behaviour that night at the club or outside the sorority house would only come under scrutiny with the benefit of hindsight. Bundy's behaviour may have created a sense of unease in certain perceptive individuals, but none of it would have been enough to raise immediate or extreme concern that he was about to commit a heinous and bloody act.

And so, when he slipped out of the club after 3am and followed some of the sorority sisters home then made his way across the path to the house where they slept, there was nothing in place to stop him. He hid in the bushes, cradling a thick wooden log made of oak in his hands.

Within minutes, he was inside the house and behind closed doors with a group of young students who still had their whole lives ahead of them and had never for a second supposed that they were unsafe at the university.

Nobody heard anything, nobody saw anything, but Bundy let his demons loose and served his most base desires as freely as he could. Eventually, it would fall to a young student and sorority sister named Nita Neary to figure out the shocking truth that something highly suspicious was unfolding in the sorority house.

At around 3.15am, she finally got home and said goodbye to her date at the back door, and then hurried inside as it was a cold winter night.

As she made her way through the living room to the front entrance hall, she heard footsteps coming down the stairs. When she reached the hall, she saw a man standing at the front door, completely out of place. Furthermore, he was holding a club in his right hand and had his left hand on the doorknob, preparing to leave. Nita caught a glimpse of his right profile for several seconds before he exited. That image would be forever printed on her mind and later become a key element of her testimony.

But for now, she was left wondering how to go about sharing what she had just seen.

She went upstairs to her room and woke her roommate to tell her that she had just seen a male intruder leaving the house. She described him, noting that he wore light-coloured pants, a dark jacket and a skiing cap. He had a protruding nose and carried a large stick wrapped in cloth.

They wanted to act quickly, so Nita raced upstairs to wake her roommate, Nancy Dowdy. The two spoke hurriedly and quickly agreed they should check the front door and lock it in case he came back. This they did and, finding nobody downstairs, headed to the room of their sorority president. She came out into the hall to talk to them when suddenly, another sorority sister named Karen Chandler opened her door and staggered down the hall.

At first Nancy thought she might be drunk or sick, but when she saw her face, she was horrified to see her bleeding profusely and holding her one arm with her other arm. Her jaw was badly broken, her skull was fractured, and both her arm and her finger had been broken too.

She was too shocked to speak clearly, but the sorority sisters were able to ascertain that she'd likely been brutally attacked by the intruder who had recently left.

Nancy took Karen to a bed while the others called for emergency services and the police. And from there, they took stock and realized the brutal reality of what had just unfolded very quickly inside their home.

Karen's roommate Kathy Kleiner was found sitting on her bed in total shock and with extremely severe injuries. She had been so savagely attacked that her jaw, broken in three places, was only just still attached to her skull on one side.

Merely minutes before the other sorority sisters were to find them in this state, Kathy had been woken up by the sound of someone entering their room and tripping over their stuff in the dark room. She'll never forget the sight of that dark silhouette hovering over her bed, nor the feeling of a heavy log being smashed down on her head. The blow was so strong that it initially felt like just a dull thud; however, the pain quickly became excruciating across her whole body as he shattered her jaw and ripped open her cheek, nearly severing her tongue.

After attacking Kathy, Bundy turned his attention to Karen, who was also in the room. He began to strike her with the same log, which gave Kathy the chance to hide in case he turned his attention back to her. The attack left Kathy with severe injuries: her jaw was broken in three places, several teeth were shattered, and she had deep lacerations on her face.

Nita and the others were in utter shock and disbelief at seeing their sorority sisters in this state. And many had now gathered in the common rooms of the house, including sorority sister Terri Murphy, who had served Bundy at her earlier shift at the bar.

But the worst was yet to come.

Within just a few minutes, as the sorority sisters began checking up on all of the young women in the house that night – around thirty in total – they discovered the bodies of two beloved housemates, Margaret Bowman and Lisa Levy.

After entering through the back door with the faulty lock, Bundy had crept into Margaret's room, where he bludgeoned her with the oak log before strangling her with pantihose. The beating was so severe that he had crushed her skull, inflicted other injuries too, and left her for dead. She would succumb to her injuries before any help arrived.

As soon as that was done, he had made his way into Lisa's room and brutally beat her unconscious with the same log that he had used to attack Margaret. After this savage attack, and in dead silence, he sexually assaulted her with a hairspray bottle and then strangled her and bit her. She was found with significant injuries, including a crushed skull and bite marks that would later become crucial evidence. Emergency responders initially detected a heartbeat when they found her, but she ultimately died from her injuries shortly after being transported to the hospital.

Both women were attacked while they were asleep, meaning they were unable to try and defend themselves, and the nature of their injuries indicates that they experienced significant trauma before dying.

While the majority of Bundy's victims died at his hands, the survivors were at least able to give the world a sense of their full lives and the minutiae of their daily existence, and in doing so, preserve the humanity of the victims, both living and dead, and a sense of them as ordinary people whose lives were cut short.

On the day before Bundy went on the rampage in the Chi Omega house, Karen had visited her parents. They lived in Tallahassee, and on the Saturday morning, many hours before the brutal attacks, her father phoned her to say her mother had bad flu.

Her father asked if she wouldn't mind coming to visit and preparing a dinner for them.

"My dad actually wanted me to stay, but I had a project due on Monday that I needed to work on so I went back to the sorority house," Karen would later describe.

She arrived back between 9pm and 10pm, chatting to a few of her sorority sisters who were watching television, and caught up with a few others and then brushed her teeth and went to her room to work on her project.

Her roommate Kathy had been at a wedding that day and came home around 11pm.

It was around 11.30pm when they switched their lights off and fell asleep in their single twin beds with the wooden trunk between them in the middle.

Then, as always, the two girls slept soundly in their beds without a care in the world other than the usual facets of student life – academic projects, social dynamics, arrangements for the next day …

Kathy would later recall, "That night, I heard the door swish open against the carpet and I woke up. I heard this loud noise of someone kicking the foot locker we had between our beds. I open my eyes but the room is so dark and all I see is a silhouette of someone standing right next to my bed. He raised his arm up over my head, and he had something in his hand, and it turned out to be a log, an oak log from outside. He hit me so hard on my face that at first it didn't hurt. It was like just a thud. Then within seconds, the pain was excruciating."

Kathy then witnessed Bundy turning on her roommate.

Now Kathy tried to cry for help, but couldn't.

"I was moaning and groaning and I thought I was yelling and screaming for help but all I was doing was making gurgling sounds from all the blood in my mouth. He came back over to my side of the room so I tucked myself into the smallest ball. I thought if he didn't see me, he wouldn't kill me."

Then the chance arrival of a car outside would spook the killer.

"He looked at me. He raised his arm up over his head, but just as he was about to hit me again, a bright light shone through our window. Our window faced the back parking lot and we always kept our curtains open. He got real antsy and started moving around. Then he ran out of the room."

The car lights that shone through the window were likely those of a car dropping a sorority sister off after a date and a night on the town.

"He didn't get to go down that hall and kill more women. That light saved my life," she said.

Neither Karen nor Kathy would be able to provide any description of their assailant as they were attacked in their sleep.

But while all of this chaos was unfolding, and police and emergency services were swarming around the Chi Omega sorority, Ted was still actively in some frenzied bloodlust. He headed off in search of another victim, having left two girls dead, two severely injured, and scores of others in a state of shock and grief.

Just a few blocks away, at around 4am, in a duplex near the university campus, he entered through the window of an apartment in a duplex. Two neighbours heard loud noises coming from the neighbouring apartment and promptly called their next-door neighbour, Cheryl Thomas, who was a dance major at the university, to see what all the noise was about. Uncharacteristically, she did not respond, which gave them a sense that something was wrong, so they called the police. When they got there, the police entered the apartment and found Cheryl lying severely beaten in her bed. She too had been attacked while sleeping and was unable to describe or identify her assailant. In the room, they discovered a knotted pair of pantihose that did not belong to Cheryl, with holes in the fabric suggesting it may have been used as a mask.

Cheryl's jaw was broken in two places and a nerve leading to her left ear was severed. This would ultimately result in lifelong hearing loss and balance issues, but for now, it was just a miracle that she had survived, and this was thanks to the quick-thinking friend and neighbour, Debbie Ciccarelli. She was the one who had called the police, who were able to get to Cheryl so quickly.

Why would someone who was on the run after escaping from prison, and who had just committed heinous crimes at a high-profile sorority house minutes earlier, not flee the area in the fear of being caught? Why did he continue that night with his "hunt"?

It is possible that this pattern of escalating violence was due to a frenzied state, driven by his compulsion to kill. But circumstances had also played in Bundy's favour. When he fled the sorority house and was back out in the quiet night, he simply looked over at Cheryl's apartment and calculated that he could break in without arousing suspicion, and for the most part, that's what he did.

His history of violent behaviour had already shown that he had an extremely strong, overwhelming compulsion to attack women, and his actions on that cold early morning in Tallahassee suggest that he felt an uncontrollable urge to continue his rampage after experiencing the thrill of his earlier attacks.

Interestingly, however, the attack on Cheryl also shows that he had become far less organized and methodical in his approach. Ted was a man who prided himself on his work, on leaving no clues behind and spending time doing his research. These attacks were not that. Some law enforcement experts noted that Bundy's method of operation appeared disorganized during this period, possibly due to stress from being on the run. This disorganization may have led him to act impulsively, seeking out victims in a more opportunistic manner rather than adhering to his usual patterns of careful planning.

But what is even more chilling than the fact that he immediately sought another potential victim after leaving Chi

Omega is how he behaved moments later, once he was back at The Oak wearing a calm exterior and playing the role of the concerned community member.

Between 4am and 5am that morning, 15 January 1978, two men who knew Ted Bundy from The Oak rooming house arrived home. As they entered, they noticed Bundy standing outside, gazing towards the Florida State University campus, where the recent crimes had occurred. The men greeted him casually, but Bundy did not respond. It was almost like he was trying to relive the moments that had occurred only hours earlier.

Later that day, around noon, several residents of The Oak, including Bundy, were discussing the news of the attacks. During this conversation, one witness suggested that the perpetrator was "some lunatic" who was likely hiding out in fear. Bundy disagreed, asserting that the crimes were "a professional job" and that the killer was someone experienced who had probably already left the area.

Little did the two men know just how experienced the Chi Omega killer was and that, as they spoke to him on that early morning about the brutal attacks nearby, they were looking into the eyes of the man who had done them.

16

The Final Horror

Unbelievably, only three weeks after the Chi Omega murders that had stunned the nation, Ted Bundy was back in a white van and driving around Florida looking for new opportunities to kill. He arrived in the town of Jacksonville and pulled into a local shopping centre parking lot from where he could observe young girls and women passing by.

When he saw a young 14-year-old walking by, he made his move and approached her. But Bundy was caught by surprise when her brother suddenly appeared at her side and demanded to know what was going on. Bundy was flustered and fled the scene. Unfortunately for him, this time he had targeted the children of a Detective Parmenter of the Jacksonville Police Department. These children had grown up conditioned on how to respond during a crime and they were able to keep their wits about them and record the licence plate number of the unmarked white van as Bundy drove away from the scene of his attempted abduction.

The children wasted no time in reporting what had just happened. When the police looked up the licence tag, they soon discovered that the white van had been stolen from a

Tallahassee residence near the Chi Omega sorority house on 13 January 1978, the day of the attack. The police seized on this detail and tried to get as much information as they could from the children. They even went so far as to hypnotize the children shortly after this incident, according to a later appeal filed before the Florida Supreme Court: "At the suggestion of Leon County authorities, Detective Parmenter agreed to have his children hypnotized. After the hypnotic session, each child was asked to separately make a police composite of the man they had seen on February 8, 1978. These composites were introduced into evidence at trial. Later, during a photo review conducted by the Leon County Sheriff's Department, both Parmenter children picked out the picture of Bundy as the man they confronted on February 8, 1978, with the white van."

Police in Jacksonville went on high alert but to no avail. Bundy's sixth sense told him that it was no longer safe for him in that city, so he headed west for 60 miles until he came to the town of Lake City, Florida. It was the kind of town where everyone knew each other, people made lifelong friendships and crime was so rare that keys were often just left in cars with the doors unlocked.

Ted checked in to a Holiday Inn and had an early night. But the very next day, he resumed his wicked mission. It was a miserable day in the Sunshine State. Grey skies and a steady drizzle hung over the town all day. Bundy drove around looking for opportunities until he happened upon Lake City Junior High School, where 12-year-old Kimberly Leach was a seventh-grade student. She was a beautiful young girl with striking features, a wide, open, friendly face, and dark hair parted in the middle. Her classmate Sheri Roberts McKinley said Kim was "very shy". On that particular school day, Kim was supposed to meet up with her friend Lisa Little, who told ABC News, "I went to our designated spot to meet up to go to our class together and she wasn't there."

None of the school authorities realized Kimberly was missing until she was called to the office to retrieve an item of hers that had been left lying around. When she didn't show up, they did a sweep of the grounds and discovered that the child was missing. Immediately, a search was initiated.

Earlier that day, Clarence Anderson, a firefighter who had been returning home, had noticed a man and a young girl walking across the campus towards a white van. He simply assumed that they were related and that the child was being taken home by her father because she was ill or had been misbehaving and didn't think about it again for months.

The frantic search for Kimberly consumed the school community but it yielded no results at all. She had simply vanished into thin air. It would be another eight weeks before Kimberly's small, battered body was found under a hog pen in a wooded area in Suwannee River State Park. She had been sexually assaulted before being murdered. "She must've been horrified and so scared," her friend McKinley said. "You don't understand. Even when you hear the details, you can't comprehend it as being a 12-year-old and this is your classmate, who was just innocent."

As soon as he had completed his murderous tasks, Bundy fled town and, for some unknown reason, headed back to Tallahassee – the site of the Chi Omega murders. On the night of 11 February, Officer Dawes was on patrol in an unmarked car when he spotted a man acting suspiciously, trying to lock and unlock a car door. The officer parked and watched the scene for a while, then approached the man and asked to see some identification, but the man claimed he had none. The officer shone his flashlight into the car and noticed a licence plate lying on the floor of the car. Dawes instructed the man to stay where he was, then returned to his police car to run a radio check on the plates, only to discover that they matched the plates reported by the Parmenter children. But when he returned to make an arrest, he discovered that the man had fled.

At that point, Bundy realized that Florida was getting too dangerous for him, so he drove west for 200 miles towards the Louisiana state line, where he judged he would be safe from the Florida police force who were on the lookout for a lone male with murderous intent.

Thirteen miles from the border, in the town of Pensacola, Ted Bundy's luck finally ran out. Once again, it was the traffic officials who had the insight to recognize that something was off about this guy. That night, Pensacola Police Officer David Lee was working a midnight shift in the Brownsville area, and he was the one who nabbed the fugitive from justice. The Pensacola police are proud of their place in history and can justifiably claim that they were the ones who finally brought Ted Bundy to heel. The police report explains:

> While he was checking buildings, [Officer Lee] noticed a Volkswagen Beetle behind Oscar's Restaurant on West Cervantes Street. Almost immediately, the driver pulled the car onto Cervantes and drove to "W" Street, where he turned North with Officer Lee behind him. Lee ran a check on the tag and discovered that the Volkswagen had been reported stolen. Lee pulled it over outside city limits at W and Cross streets near Catholic High School. He ordered the driver out of the car and made him lie down. When Lee approached, the man attacked him and tried to take his gun. It was necessary for Officer Lee to use force to subdue the man. He was then placed under arrest and taken to the Pensacola Police headquarters.

Bundy knew that he was in real trouble when he was pulled over, and he knew that it would take all of his considerable charm to be able to talk himself out of this situation. He was also certain there was no way he could allow himself to be arrested in Florida, so moments before the officer read him his rights, he desperately lunged for the officer's gun and the two men fell to the ground wrestling. Officer Lee was able to get control, and he struck Bundy in the face with the barrel of the gun, then placed him in handcuffs and threw him into the back of the police car. But at that point, he had no idea who he had pulled in. To him, it was just another man who had made a few bad choices.

Also on duty that night was Inspector Norman Chapman, who had only been with the department for three years. It felt like a routine arrest when Bundy was brought in. "He was very personable, very charismatic, very unalarming, and see, that's the dangerous thing," Chapman said. His suspicions were aroused when the accused was booked in at the station and it was discovered that Bundy was carrying 21 stolen credit cards, many of which belonged to FSU students.

Down at the station, Bundy gave a false name, hoping that he would simply be charged for a misdemeanour and let go the following day.

He had been so close to crossing state lines and starting afresh somewhere new, but his insatiable need to keep destroying lives finally sealed his downfall. Chapman told a local news station on the 40th anniversary of the arrest that Bundy was very nearly able to cross state lines and get away. "He had actually left Pensacola on his way to Mobile, when he got the urge to take another person," Chapman said. "So he came in the last exit, came back into Pensacola and he stopped behind Oscar Woerner's."

Bundy locked the car and started walking the streets, peeping in windows just like he had been doing since he was a teenager.

But his search was fruitless and he must have lost track of time because it was almost 1am when he returned to the stolen car and swung out of the parking lot in front of Officer Lee, who then pulled him over and made the arrest.

For the first few days he was detained, Bundy insisted that his name was Kenneth Misner, and he even had an ID card under that name that proved his identity. But it wasn't long before the police received a call from the real Kenneth Misner telling them he was out there living his life and he was not the guy they had in custody. Bundy was forced to admit that the driver's licence and ID he was carrying were fake, but he still refused to give them his real name, which led to a circuit court judge ordering him to be detained without bond.

The charges against him were listed as possession of stolen property, including a car, a television, credit cards and false automobile tags, as well as battery of a police officer and resisting arrest. In Bundy's court appearance to answer these charges, the opposing counsel argued over whether he deserved to get a bond or not. The judge in the case became visibly frustrated by the defendant's refusal to disclose his identity and summed up what most people were feeling when he said, "Until we find out who he is, there is no way we can bail him out."

Without a name or an identity to work with, the investigators turned their attention to the car he was driving and soon discovered that it had been stolen from a location in Tallahassee very near the Chi Omega house around the time of the murders. Their prisoner was becoming more and more interesting to them.

The cat-and-mouse game with police and detectives was taking its toll on Bundy. In order to keep his identity hidden, he had not made contact with a single person from his life, and it was that sense of total isolation that eventually wore him down. Finally, he admitted that he just needed to talk to someone from his old life, someone who was not out to get him, so eventually he gave up this charade and told investigators that he would admit his identity in exchange for a phone call to his ex-girlfriend Liz Kloepfer. "I needed a friend," he said. "I needed somebody to talk to who would help me get over the reaction that I was having to being back in custody." It's interesting that the person he called when he got offered that first phone call was Liz Kloepfer and not Carole Ann Boone.

In fact, Carole was only the fifth person that he called over the following days. Bundy's phone calls revealed his true priorities. He reached out first to Liz, then his mother and his longtime friend Marlin Vortman, then sought counsel from Seattle attorney John Henry Browne. Only after these calls did he contact Carole Boone – a telling detail for a woman who believed she held a singular place in his life. After all, she was the one who had sacrificed so much for him, who had maintained that he was innocent and believed in him all along. Meanwhile, unbeknownst to Ted, Liz was the one who had first given his name to the authorities all those years ago.

Speaking in the 2020 documentary *Falling for a Killer*, Liz recognized in Carole Ann Boone the same vulnerability Bundy had once exploited in her. "I felt like she was going to be roped in just like I was," she said. "This isn't going to end well for her. He'd spent a lifetime observing women, and deciding who was going to become a victim. I think he could tell when women had the codependence issue, where they wanted to help him in any way they could."

When Kloepfer was interviewed by the police following her conversation with Bundy, the details were chilling. She explained how the first time he called her up, he was still defensive and evasive, and his chief concern was to try and counter all the bad things that he knew she would be hearing about him over the next few days. But he refused to discuss why he had been arrested, and he became withdrawn and angry when she asked him point blank if his arrest had anything to do with the killing of those sorority girls in Tallahassee. The next day he reached his breaking point. He called Liz back and admitted out loud, probably for the first time in his whole life, that "he was sick and that he was consumed by something that he didn't understand and that he just couldn't contain it."

Later, while speaking about himself in the third person to journalist Stephen Michaud, Bundy was able to provide key insights and a window into why he kept killing over and over again. "Perhaps [this person] hoped that through this violent series of acts, which every murder leaving a person of this type hungry, unfulfilled, would leave him with an obviously irrational belief that the next time he did it he would be fulfilled, or the next time he did it he would be fulfilled, or the next time."

With that kind of psychotic hunger driving him, there was no way that Bundy was ever going to simply quit what he was doing and choose a normal life. It was too big and overpowering for him, and he could not control these urges. The only way that this was ever going to end was with Bundy being murdered by someone he was attacking or being caught and locked away for life. Those were the only options. Nothing else would prove strong enough to stop him.

Six weeks after he escaped detention in Colorado, Ted Bundy was back behind bars for the last time. That night in Pensacola would be the last time he ever walked the streets alone after dark, peering in windows and hunting for innocent victims. The long national nightmare of a psychopathic killer travelling unimpeded across the United States raping, terrorizing and murdering young women at will was drawing to a close. There were three young women who would still be alive if the authorities in Colorado had been able to keep Bundy behind bars, and two others who would carry injuries from his attacks for the rest of their lives. Armed with the knowledge of how devious he was, the cops in Florida put him in maximum security and made sure that they did not make the same mistake as their colleagues up north had made.

In prison, Bundy was outraged at the charges against him, writing in a letter that betrayed how victimized he felt to a journalist. "Nothing I do can possibly be interpreted innocently, can it? If, on the day after the murders, I had picked up and fled Tallahassee, you and everyone else would be asking: Well, if you weren't guilty, why didn't you stick around, you didn't have anything to be afraid of, did you? I didn't have anything to fear. I was not responsible for what happened at Chi Omega, I didn't do it, I wasn't there, so there was no reason for me to suspect that my presence alone would be sufficient to indict me for something I was innocent of. I am discouraged by human nature, yours included, as it applies to my case, because no matter what I say or do at this point, I am damned if I do and damned if I don't."

17

The Chi Omega Trials

The long-awaited moment finally arrived on a hot and humid summer day in Miami, Florida, in 1979: Ted Bundy would stand trial in a court of law for the crime of murder. He had escaped judgement in Colorado by fleeing before he could stand trial for the murder of Caryn Campbell in a case he may well have won. Now, he was accused of the brutal murders of two women, Lisa Levy and Margaret Bowman, at the Chi Omega sorority house at Florida State University, as well as the attempted murders of Kathy Kleiner and Karen Chandler, both of whom had been severely injured and left for dead.

The case against him here was far stronger, and it's fair to say that he must have wondered if he should have taken his chances with that case in a state that was far more reluctant to impose the death penalty. Between 1975 and 2020, Colorado only put one man, Gary Davis, to death in 1997. Over the same time frame, Florida executed over 100.

Apart from the obvious news buzz around a notorious criminal going on trial for murder, there was another key aspect that would shape American life going forward: this was to be a televised trial laid bare for all of the American public to experience as it was happening.

The decision to allow cameras in Bundy's courtroom was made by the Florida Supreme Court on 1 May 1979, just a month before the trial began. This ruling that permitted extensive media coverage led to an influx of journalists and camera crews from across the country and around the world. Over 250 reporters attended the trial from all the states across America and from nine other countries, and it was broadcast live on several networks, making it accessible to millions of viewers.

Reflecting on the trial in *Conversations with a Killer*, Ed Hula, Florida PBS correspondent, says, "The lurid nature of the case, the depravity of the violence and the personality of Ted Bundy combined to make this something the media could not ignore."

And once they were inside, each figure in this real-life courtroom drama became a "character" that journalists could fix their gaze upon as the proceedings unfolded.

One such "character" was Judge Edward Cowart. Known for his Southern charm and calm demeanour, his handling of the trial, balancing professionalism and sternness, often became a focus of media attention. But what really stood out was that his grounded-ness and authenticity stood in sharp contrast to the man on trial.

With the cameras rolling, Bundy was all charisma and theatrics. On the first day, he arrived in a stone-coloured suit with his dark wavy hair neatly framing his face, and he seemed to lap up the cameras all around him.

While those at home could feast on the spectacle from the comfort of their own couches thanks to the televising of the trial, others arrived in droves outside the courthouse each day. Bundy even developed a following of admirers, particularly young women, who sent him letters and religiously attended the trial.

It did not take long before the first shock of the trial, which arrived when Bundy blindsided his own counsel on the very first day.

Michael Minerva had been appointed to represent Bundy, and before the trial began, he came to the conclusion that a plea deal would be the most favourable outcome for Bundy. In such a deal, in light of the overwhelming evidence, Bundy would plead guilty in exchange for a 75-year prison sentence and be spared the electric chair, and for all intents and purposes, he had told his counsel he would take it.

The prosecution and the defence both arrived in court that morning confident that Bundy would be admitting to the murders and saving his own life in the process. In this instance, the trial would be over very quickly.

Perhaps it was the presence of the cameras that made Bundy opt for a long and drawn-out case. Instead of admitting guilt, Bundy stood up and started making a speech before the judge.

"It's my position that my counsel, one, believe that I am guilty. Two, that they have told me they see no way of presenting effective defense, and in no uncertain terms they have told me that. And three, that they see no way of avoiding conviction," he proclaimed.

Minerva sat dumbstruck and embarrassed as Bundy threw him under the bus in front of the judge and the massive television audience.

Bundy continued, "Your Honour, if that does not raise itself to the level of ineffectiveness of counsel, I don't know what does."

Minerva, decades later, would recall, "He sabotaged the plea and turned it down. I mean, it was demoralizing to me."

Despite the potential benefits of accepting the plea deal, Bundy rejected it. He likely believed he could manipulate the legal system and achieve an acquittal or a more favourable outcome during the trial. His snubbing the deal might also have stemmed from his desire to maintain control over the narrative and stay in the spotlight as long as possible. Ted had always loved the glare of the media.

After firing Minerva, Bundy insisted that he would be representing himself in court. This decision was influenced by his belief that he could effectively argue his case despite lacking formal legal training. Minerva stayed on in an advisory role, but Bundy's insistence on self-representation created significant challenges during the trial.

On the one hand, it allowed him a platform to showcase his intelligence and manipulative abilities, but on the other, his performance as his own attorney was so erratic and theatrical that those not fascinated with him were disgusted by him. But his real downfall came during cross-examinations, where his performance was often inadequate and revealed gaps in his legal knowledge.

These played right into the hands of state prosecutor Larry Simpson who would later say in *Conversations with a Killer*, "Nobody knew for sure that we were going to get a conviction, ultimately, in trial. But the one thing that we were absolutely positive of was that we did not want Mr Bundy back on the streets again."

After Minerva ceased to lead the defence, another court-appointed attorney, Margaret Good, joined.

Good was in her early thirties at the time and was, in fact, just a few days younger than Bundy himself. Reflecting on that moment in her life, she would later say, "I was just a run-of-the-mill, idealistic, young criminal defence lawyer. When asked to do a very difficult job, I said, 'Yes, I'll do it.'"

But Good had reservations about Bundy being on his own defence team.

"We took the position that Ted was incompetent. He didn't understand the evidence against him. It's a basic principle of our law that you don't try a person when they are incompetent."

A competency hearing then followed and, as Good recalls, still surprised decades later, "The judge, remarkably, ruled that he was competent. Judge Cowart ruled that not only was Ted competent to stand trial but that he would be in charge of his own defence."

This was, in her words, "just a very difficult situation because there were times when he was very erratic, impulsive and strange".

She said the team behind Bundy could not control his impulses and his irrationality any more than he could and that it was "annoying and it was different and we had no training in how to handle it".

Among the more bizarre moments were when Bundy, when asked by Judge Cowart what he sought, said he needed daily outdoor exercise. He also asked for more access to the jail's law library and the use of a typewriter. He also complained about the poor lighting in his cell, saying it hindered his ability to read and thus help his defence team, and that prompted the judge to check the situation himself during a recess and then provide Bundy with an alternative location in which to read with better lighting.

Simpson would later recall, "One of my favourite motions that he filed was a motion for a change of menu, arguing that he had eaten the same grilled cheese sandwich every day for the last five or six days and that he just really needed something else."

A more crass situation you could not find: a serial killer asking for more exercise opportunities, nicer food and a typewriter, when everyone in the courtroom was made privy to the utter force he had used to snuff out the life of his victims using a tree club.

With this as the backdrop, by far the most disturbing spectacle during the trial was when Bundy cross-examined the first responders who arrived at Chi Omega and bore witness to the extreme injuries that had killed Lisa Levy and Margaret Bowman.

Bundy seemed almost eager and titillated as he questioned police officer Ray Crew and the medical personnel. His voice was calm and steady as he pushed them to recall the brutal details of what they'd found.

Bundy leaned forward and asked specific, disturbing questions about what they had seen when they first entered the sorority house.

It soon became quite clear to anyone in the courtroom: he wasn't looking to prove his innocence so much as he was dragging out each grim detail into the light. Through very pointed questions, he coaxed the responders into describing the positioning of the victims' bodies, the bloodstains on the wall and the injuries each woman had suffered. Officers and paramedics shifted uncomfortably in their seats as they tried to keep their answers straightforward and clinical, avoiding Bundy's gaze.

But at one point, he even interrupted one witness to correct a minor detail, displaying his authority on the crime scene.

If his perverted enjoyment was stimulated by hearing these details now recounted under his own direction, it certainly didn't help his case. It was as though he were revisiting the murders, pulling memories out of the witnesses and savouring their discomfort.

Throughout this cross-examination, the courtroom remained tense and people watched, horrified, as he orchestrated a retelling of the details of that night, but most bizarrely, even this did not deter some of his "fans", who passed notes to Good to pass on to Bundy or sat with their eyes glued to him in the courtroom, and certainly, it did not deter Carole Ann Boone.

She had become a feature of the trial in her own right. In the definitive profile of Carole Ann on the *Killer in the Archives* blog, the author writes:

> By the summer of 1979, Carole had quit her job in Washington to join Ted full-time in Florida, living in cheap motels near the jail and working 18 hours a day on his defense. "She basically became his legal secretary. I could tell that she had clerical abilities, somebody who could keep files and keep organized," remembered Rich Bundy. When the *Orlando Sentinel* asked her for comment during the Chi Omega murder trial in Miami, she claimed that Bundy's problems began in 1975, when "a bitter and angry ex-girlfriend [Liz Kloepfer] phoned authorities in Washington state, establishing a tenuous thread between Ted and the murders of two women [at Lake Sammamish] there. The rest is history."

As the bizarre trial wore on, it eventually came time for Chi Omega's Nita Neary to give evidence. Just 21 years old and steadfastly unshaken by Bundy's presence in court, she walked up to the stand, perhaps feeling the weight of the whole sorority on her shoulders. Like all the others in the house during the attack, Nita was keenly aware that it had been purely random who got killed, raped or left for dead on that awful morning, and it could as easily have been her as it was her friends Lisa, Margaret, Kathy and Karen. Now, here she was, in front of a judge, jury, and curious public with countless television lenses trained on her. She had the awesome power to testify and dole out revenge on the man who had upended so many lives and send him to the electric chair, and she did not hesitate to take her chance.

Simpson and his team did not have strong physical forensic evidence lifted at the crime scene, so Nita's testimony would soon prove invaluable.

She described the man she'd seen at the front door of the Chi Omega house as having a very prominent nose with a straight bridge that almost came to a point. She said he had thin lips and was clean-shaven.

When Simpson asked her if that man was in the courtroom, she very stridently raised her arm and pointed her hand in his direction. He felt assured by her testimony, and recalled, "I thought that she gave a very compelling testimony, and one of the most important pieces of evidence in my mind was that she'd sat down with an artist and she described the profile view of the man. You can hold that sketch up next to Mr Bundy, and it is a spitting image of Mr Bundy."

Then it was the defence's chance to cross-examine Nita and this fell to Robert Haggard, one of the chief lawyers on Bundy's team. He threw questions at Nita that highlighted how fleeting the moment had been in which she observed the intruder at the Chi Omega house. He asked if she saw his eyes, made eye contact, saw his hair, or his ears, for that matter.

The answer to all of these questions was no.

Even so, Simpson felt she'd been a very strong witness, but Good felt otherwise, and was shocked by what Bundy did in response to that key moment in court.

"Bob Haggard did an excellent job on cross-examination. Her testimony was not very certain. And right after Robert Haggard did that very, very excellent cross-examination destroying the state's case, Ted got up in open court and tried to fire Haggard as his attorney," Good recalled on the Netflix show *Conversations with a Killer*.

Instead of letting the moment sit with the jury and settle in their minds, with the potential being that they would see Nita's testimony as being weak, Bundy seemed almost envious of Haggard's cross-examination skills and promptly said, "Attempts by me to participate in the courtroom have been met with vigorous opposition from a part of my counsel. We are speaking more to a problem that attorneys have of giving up power. Maybe we're dealing with a problem of professional psychology, where the attorneys are so jealous of the power they exercise in the courtroom, they're afraid to share it with the defendant."

With that, Haggard rose from his chair, gave no explanation, and simply walked out of the Ted Bundy murder trial, never to return.

Judge Cowart commented wryly, "And then there were three."

Haggard's departure was significant as it left the remaining attorneys, including Margaret Good, to fill in gaps that he had been preparing for. Ultimately, Bundy got what he wanted – a more prominent role in his defence after Haggard left, but this only added to the chaos of the trial.

Then came the most damning piece of evidence, and with it, the grim reality that Bundy had bitten at least one of his victims. This fact had come to light through the work of the authorities in Leon County, where the sheriff, Ken Katsaris, had been tireless in his search to uncover every possible clue.

He had shown excellent leadership during the chaotic aftermath of the Chi Omega murders, and he was instrumental in coordinating the multi-agency response to the university murders. Ultimately, it was under his watch that critical forensic evidence was collected, including the barbaric bite marks that

Bundy left on victim Lisa Levy. Katsaris felt this was a golden opportunity for the prosecution and he relished the fact that Bundy, who was both cocky and complacent in the courtroom, was about to be shown that he was not going to get away with murder as he imagined he would.

The bite mark represented the first time that such a piece of evidence would be used in a court setting.

"There was a very large, very imprinted double bite mark. The person bit, withdrew, and … bit again, as hard as the person could," recalled Katsaris.

The expert who would join the dots in the public's collective gaze was Richard Souviron, a forensic odontologist from Miami. While Bundy was awaiting trial a few weeks earlier, he had been taken off to a medical facility and forced to consent to a dental mould being made of his teeth. Once he was up on the witness stand, Dr Souviron produced a small white bundle and carefully opened it up with everyone in the courtroom spellbound.

From it he produced what he called "a stone cast of Mr Bundy's upper teeth".

He showed the cast while describing what he saw, 'the slightly crooked upper front teeth with distinct incisors and chip marks", and added, in reference to an image of the actual bite marks on Lisa Levy's body, "whoever made this mark in the skin, in the flesh, had crooked teeth".

Footage of the trial shows a dark cloud descending over Bundy as this evidence was presented. Up until then, one could see his arrogance at almost any moment in the courtroom: smirking, joking, insulting his own counsel, addressing the judge as if he were a buddy …

But with the bite mark moment came a much more worried-looking Bundy, and in his tape-recorded interviews with journalist Stephen Michaud, Bundy said, "I felt the tide turn right there … I was feeling embittered and persecuted. I couldn't endure this humiliation. I had to make a statement."

That "statement" came in the form of Bundy not showing up for court the next day and the judge being told that the guards could not get him up and that he'd jammed the lock of his cell with wet toilet paper.

This response was a direct result of him finally being cornered by the combination of Nita's testimony and that of the forensic odontologist, and when he finally arrived, Judge Cowart warned him that he could be held in contempt of court for refusing to show up. Bundy, in the true style of a narcissist, then tried to flip the script and accused the personnel in the jail of treating him in a way that amounted to harassment.

These tactics were distracting and annoying, but they did not change the fact that the trial was proceeding to its conclusion. Eventually, the moment came for the drama to end and a verdict to be delivered. The public, for the first time, had been privy to exactly the same machinations of the courtroom drama as the jury, and everyone had an opinion on what would happen next.

Those men and women of the jury who would decide Bundy's fate disappeared behind the door, where they deliberated for almost seven hours before emerging in front of the hungry row of cameras and public scrutiny once again with a decision.

Ted Bundy was found guilty of the Chi Omega murders, attempted murder of other sorority sisters and other related charges. He was sentenced to death by electric chair at Florida State Prison. In the final moments of what had been an unprecedented judicial fiasco, Judge Cowart – far from displaying disgust at Bundy's crimes – instead chose the role of the disappointed father. "Take care of yourself, young man," Cowart said. "I say that to you sincerely – take care of yourself. It is a tragedy for this court to see such a total waste, I think, of humanity that I've experienced in this court. You're a bright young man. You would have made a good lawyer and I would have loved to have you practise in front of me – but you went another way, partner."

And with that, Ted Bundy was finally plucked out of the society that he had terrorized once and for all. Never again would he be free to prowl the streets looking for lives he could cut short for his own twisted pleasure.

18

The Noose Tightens

Ted Bundy was found guilty of the Chi Omega murders on 24 July 1979 and sentenced to die in an electric chair at Florida State Prison. But this was not the end of Bundy's time in the courtroom. A year earlier, he had also been charged with the killing of Kimberly Leach, and it had been agreed by all the concerned parties that this case would proceed once the Chi Omega trial was concluded, regardless of the verdict that had been reached.

So, six months after a sentence of death had been passed on him, Ted found himself back in the dock and facing another judge, another jury and another murder trial. Bundy had resorted to his now well-worn playbook – he managed to win a change of venue, arguing that he would not be able to get a fair trial in Suwannee County, and proceedings were moved to the city of Orlando, Florida.

The media frenzy that had accompanied the Chi Omega trial was noticeably absent during the second murder trial. There was still a lot of interest in the case, but the sentence of death in the initial trial had satisfied many curious onlookers who were satisfied that justice would be done. The coverage was far less sensational compared to the Chi Omega trial. This shift allowed for a more focused discussion on forensic evidence rather than just Bundy's personality or courtroom antics.

It was a slightly more traditional trial than the one that preceded it, although Bundy did his best to inject a sense of theatricality into the proceedings. One of the most difficult aspects of the trial proved to be the selection of an impartial jury. Since coverage of the first trial had been so widespread and sensationalist, it proved extremely difficult to find ordinary citizens who would qualify as impartial jurors in this case.

The *Capital Punishment in Context* blog writes, "Under the Sixth Amendment to the Constitution, every defendant is entitled to a trial by an impartial jury of his or her peers. Due to extensive media coverage, jury selection in a high profile case can be extremely difficult. Jurors will likely have developed some biases about the case based on the media coverage to which they have been exposed."

In the case of death-qualified jurors, meaning jurors who are able to fairly consider both execution and life in prison without strong predispositions towards either, research shows that these people are even "more susceptible to pre-trial publicity than other jurors".

Slow jury selection, coupled with Bundy's attempts to change venue and drag out proceedings, did slow it down and did produce a change of venue, but ultimately the trial got underway on 7 January 1980. This time, Bundy decided to hand responsibility for his case over to defence attorneys Julius Africano and Lynn Thompson. For the prosecution, George Dekle led the team in his first murder prosecution, alongside an attorney called Jerry Blair.

Ted's defence team did not have much to work with, but they settled on a strategy of pleading not guilty by reason of insanity. Considering everything that had come to light about their client, insanity seemed like a reasonable pitch to make to a jury and a public who had come to believe that Ted Bundy was some kind of monster.

His behaviour in court during the second trial served only to reinforce the basis of his defence. Gone was the suave, cool exterior that had made him such a magnetic TV presence during the first trial. Bundy seemed to have finally gotten the picture that things were going very, very badly for him and that he was not in a position to save himself at the last minute, as had happened time and again for most of his 33 years on earth. He was increasingly unable to control his emotions. At one point in the trial, he stood up and started screaming at one of the witnesses who he disagreed with. The effort of maintaining his carefully crafted persona – the articulate, charming law student – now appeared to be draining him visibly. Every calculated smile, every measured response seemed to cost him tremendous psychological effort, as though the mask he'd worn for so many years was finally beginning to crack. Biographers Michaud and Aynesworth wrote in their book that Ted was "expending huge amounts of energy just to keep from blowing apart".

Another interesting aspect to consider in this second trial is that Bundy was far from sober for much of it, thanks to the efforts of Carole Ann Boone, who had started to spike his drinks with alcohol and lace his food with tranquillizers in an effort to keep him calm during the trial. There's a passage in the *Killer in the Archives* blog where the investigator for Bundy's defence, Don Kennedy, recalled many years later, "There were a couple occasions when Ted became intoxicated. I observed Ted thick-tongued, with slurred speech and unusual behavior. I suspected that the juice in the large sixteen-ounce resealable can had been doctored up. I tasted it myself. There was other food she brought in, sandwiches, cookies, snacks. We found pills in his bags of goodies. I flushed them down the toilet. I think Ted was disappointed that I'd done that."

Considering that he had conducted most of his killing while drunk, it does not seem out of character that he would conduct his defence while under the influence.

As the trial proceeded during that month of January, assistant state attorney Bob Dekle presented 65 witnesses who were connected either directly or indirectly with Ted Bundy or Kimberly Leach on the day she disappeared from Lake City. Some of the evidence was controversial and was open to attack from the defence, while other parts of the state's case seemed to be utterly damning for Bundy.

When it came to eyewitness accounts of that day, the state had mixed results to offer up. They were confident in the testimony of school crossing guard Chuck Edenfield, who told the jury that he had seen a man resembling Ted Bundy driving a white van in the vicinity of the school on that day.

But when it came to witnesses who saw Bundy with Leach, the prosecution was on shakier ground. The testimony of the firefighter, Clarence Anderson, was far shakier. He had seen a man walking a young girl away from school to a van, but had only come forward to say what he had seen after he saw a TV news segment about the abduction of the young girl. The problem with that was that it only occurred in July 1978, six months after the actual abduction. As they had done in the first successful prosecution, the defence had turned to hypnosis to bolster the credibility of their witness and as a way of refreshing the witness's memory. Under hypnosis, Anderson reinforced his story and doubled down, claiming that he was certain he had seen Ted Bundy leading Kimberly Leach towards a white van parked outside Lake City Junior High on that wet, grey morning.

The defence was confident they could undercut the eyewitness accounts, dismiss what the crossing guard had seen and poke holes in the hypnosis aspects of it, but the forensic evidence would prove to be much more problematic for them. The testimony began with a manager at the Florida State University Media Center, a man called Richard Shook, who testified that in early February of the previous year, a van belonging to the Center disappeared.

When it was found and taken into custody a few days after Kim Leach had gone missing, it was processed for physical evidence. The fingerprints and soil samples found in the van were inconclusive, but the blood samples told a different story. According to a later appeal filed before the Florida Supreme Court, "Blood stains on the van's carpet were found to be group B blood. The Leach girl had that type as does over fifteen percent of the human population. In addition, analyst Mary Hinson testified that it was extremely probable that both Bundy's and Leach's clothing had come in contact with the van's carpet and that the clothing of each had probably come into contact with each other."

That evidence was damning, and there was not a lot the defence could do to counter it.

After a full month of trial proceedings, the judge asked the jury to convene and consider the evidence before them, which they did, before returning with a guilty verdict seven hours later that led to scenes of jubilation and relief among the prosecution team.

Bundy and his lawyers did not sit around licking their wounds; they wasted no time in laying an appeal. They attacked the evidence gathered under hypnosis with a series of experts who argued on appeal that, in their opinion, "Anderson should never have been hypnotized in the first place because of the lapse of time between the event he was attempting to remember and the hypnotic episodes and because of all the information he had learned about the event during that intervening period of time." Their strategy was reminiscent of the argument that had been put forward regarding Carol DaRonch, the police line-up, and the seven months that had lapsed since the incident.

That time the prosecution had prevailed, but in this case, the court sided with the defence, stating, "Hypnosis has not received sufficient general acceptance in the scientific community to give reasonable assurance that the results produced under even the best of circumstances will be sufficiently reliable to outweigh the risks of abuse and prejudice ... [U]ntil hypnosis gains general acceptance in the fields of medicine and psychiatry as a method by which memories are accurately improved without undue danger of distortion, delusion, or fantasy and until the barriers which hypnosis raises to effective cross-examination are somehow overcome, the testimony of witnesses which has been tainted by hypnosis must be excluded in criminal cases."

They did add an important caveat, however, when they concluded that hypnosis does not render a witness incompetent to testify to those facts demonstrably recalled prior to hypnosis, and so the court went on to examine whether "there was sufficient evidence, excluding the hypnotically recalled testimony, to uphold Bundy's conviction". They decided that there had only been three details that had been refreshed under hypnosis and that they were all related to items of clothing. In particular, Anderson had claimed under hypnosis that the girl had been wearing a blue sweatshirt with the number "63" or "68" on it and that part of Bundy's attire that day was a pullover sweater or shirt.

Following its deliberation, the court stated, "After a thorough examination of the record before us in this case, we feel that sufficient evidence does exist, absent the tainted testimony, upon which the jury could have based its conviction of Bundy. There is no reasonable possibility that the tainted testimony complained of might have contributed to the conviction."

Sentencing following the guilty verdict was set for 9 February 1980, which in a tragic turn of events, turned out to be two years exactly to the day that Kimberly Leach had been abducted from her school and murdered. Most trial watchers expected sentencing to be an uneventful affair, with the expectation of another death sentence to add to those of the Chi Omega murders. But Ted Bundy did not plan to go quietly. He called Carole Ann Boone to the stand to testify as a character witness. Up on the stand, she told the jury that day that Bundy "is a large part of my life. He is vital to me," and also stated under oath, "I've never seen anything in Ted that indicates any destructiveness towards any other people."

But what those assembled in the courtroom did not know was that while she was helping with his defence, Boone had also been doing research into the laws of marriage and had discovered an arcane Florida law that stated that "a public declaration, properly phrased, in an open courtroom in the presence of court officers would make the [marriage] ceremony legal".

This presented an opportunity for the couple, and they were determined to take it. Bundy seemed uncharacteristically nervous on the day of sentencing, and he was dressed in a rather formal suit with a bow tie on. While examining Carole Ann as his character witness on the stand, Ted Bundy approached her with a smile and asked, "Carole, do you want to marry me?" to which she replied, "Yes," and he responded by saying, "And I want to marry you." That was all it took for them to be legally married in the eyes of the law. The prosecution was outraged that the couple would pull this kind of a stunt on such a solemn day. Later that day, Bundy realized that he had botched his response, so he was forced to correct it under cross-examination, thus making the marriage between Bundy and Boone legal.

When challenged about his impromptu marriage proposal during proceedings – a moment that had spectators gasping and reporters scrambling – he bristled at suggestions it was mere theatre. "This wasn't for your benefit," he told the stunned jurors, his voice taking on that familiar charm. The courtroom, he insisted, had simply provided the stage for an intimate moment between lovers. "It was the only chance to be in the same room together where the right words could be said. It was something between she and I."

Carole Ann was equally indignant that anyone would question the validity of their love, telling journalists, "Ted is a major figure in my son's life; he takes a great deal of interest in Jamey and provides him with guidance and advice that a boy needs. Formalizing our relationship will be comforting to the three of us and is something that Ted and I have wanted for a long time. I know what I'm all about and I know what Ted's all about. It's a very private thing and I don't care what people external to our lives think."

As Ann Rule points out in her book, the anniversary of Kimberly Leach's death had also become the anniversary of Ted Bundy's engagement, which was another attack on the memory of that poor child. But Bundy's mini-triumph was short-lived. He had been sentenced to die for the third time in a year, and he spent his honeymoon alone and locked up on death row in Florida State's Raiford Penitentiary.

That summer of 1979, while Ted Bundy adjusted to his new life on death row, a curious nonprofit organization emerged in Washington state. It was called the Would-Be Foundation, and it was orchestrated by Carole Ann Boone and backed by Bundy's inner circle – including his mother Louise and close friend Marlin Vortman, who would both be serving as board members. On paper, the foundation was created to help indigent criminal defendants with financial support. But the reality of what it was about turned out to be far more calculated.

What it was was actually an elaborate workaround scheme designated to navigate around the newly enacted "Son of Sam" laws, which prevented criminals from profiting from their notoriety. As it turns out, a Ted Bundy book deal was in the works, and so the plan was for the foundation to serve as a legal channel for the publishing money from the book to flow indirectly to Bundy's family. The plan seemed perfect: the publisher would fund the "charitable organization", which would then distribute the proceeds to Bundy's chosen beneficiaries.

But like most of Bundy's schemes, this one unravelled quickly. During his interviews with the authors who had been commissioned to try to get unique insights into his mind, Bundy played his usual games of half-truths and manipulation. This evasive behaviour and refusal to speak frankly violated the terms of his publishing contract, and as a result the carefully constructed financial arrangement with the Would-Be Foundation collapsed. Nevertheless, when the book was published, it went on to become a *New York Times* bestseller of 1983, but Carole Ann and the Bundy hangers-on never saw a penny of that money. The Would-Be Foundation quietly disappeared into bureaucratic oblivion when Marlin Vortman failed to renew its registration, taking with it another of Bundy's carefully constructed facades.

19

Life in Prison

In the summer of 1979, Ted Bundy arrived at his final address: Florida State Prison, Raiford. The maximum security facility rises out of the flat, humid Florida landscape like an island of brick surrounded by razor wire and watchtowers. Outside its walls, the town of Raiford itself barely registers on a map – nothing more than a quiet collection of modest homes and churches that just over two hundred people call home, most of whom work at the enormous security facility that has defined this patch of Florida since 1961.

In the walls of Raiford, Ted Bundy's domain had shrunk to a single cell on death row. The man who had stalked the streets, evading police and crossing state lines with impunity, now found himself caged, his vast hunting grounds reduced to the confines of this maximum security prison.

But Bundy would not go quietly into the void. Even here, in the final stages of his life, he found a way to claim one more victim. Carole Ann Boone, the woman who had sworn her loyalty to the end, would stay inextricably bound to him until nearly the very last moment. As he eked out the last of his sad years, he pulled Boone, willingly or not, into the shadows with him until it was almost too late.

She and her son Jamey had moved to Florida during the Chi Omega trials to be with Ted and help him fight the charges against him. She had given up everything for this man and was living in such abject poverty that she was forced to move into a motel room with her son and the writer Stephen Michaud while they were working together on the Bundy book and the Would-Be Foundation, an arrangement about which Michaud would later recall with distaste. "I had no choice; she was the key to keeping Ted talking," sighed Michaud. "I shudder when I think about it. That was one of my least favorite times in my life, I'll tell you that."

Life on death row was like nothing Ted Bundy had ever experienced before. His existence had been refined down to the bare essentials. Before that point, he had worked a series of odd jobs without ever committing, been a college student for almost a decade, and had travelled extensively across the continent. Bundy had enjoyed all the friends of freedom that came with being in the privileged American middle class over the course of his lifetime, and he had lost it all. Now it was a life lived in a box with hours upon hours of nothingness. In a letter to a cousin, he described his daily routine, while still managing to give hints of the narcissism at the core of his personality by comparing himself to Mahatma Gandhi. "I live in a 9x12 foot space," he wrote. "There is a bunk and toilet and sink. We're down to basics here. I'm in the cell all day. Sometimes I run back-and-forth and do sit-ups and other exercises. Sometimes yoga. I usually take a nap around noon. I sleep well."

At least that was the official story. Behind the scenes, there was a lot more happening. For one thing, Carole Ann Boone was desperate to get pregnant and have a baby with her husband, and it was surprisingly easy to make that happen. All it took was a few illicit payments to the right prison guards. By February of 1981, she was pregnant with a child who had been conceived behind a water cooler. She later told Michaud with a laugh, "We kept looking out the window … there was a black guard who was real nice. And after the first day, they just didn't care. They even walked in on us a couple of times."

Bundy knew that one of the last valuable things that he possessed was his story, and he tried hard to leverage it to his advantage. He stated quite clearly that he would be open to telling his story in his own words on one condition: that it was accompanied by a re-examination of the case against him. Stephen Michaud had no illusions about the task he was being asked to undertake in telling this story. "I think Ted regarded me as someone to be used or manipulated in his cause."

After the book deal had been negotiated, Michaud set off for the prison, where he would spend almost one hundred hours talking with Bundy and creating the tapes that would form the basis of his bestselling book with Hugh Aynesworth and the Netflix documentary. Telling his story was one more way that Bundy was able to fill the lonely, depressing hours of prison life and shape how the world perceived him.

In 1981, the pregnant Boone and her son Jamey were able to move into a two-bedroom apartment with their own kitchen and a steady supply of hot water, which was a huge upgrade to her life and a relief to everyone involved.

Ted Bundy and Carole Ann Boone's daughter was born on 24 October 1981. They called her Rosa. It was a difficult birth but Carole Ann came through it and was determined that the father of her child would see his baby on the day that she was born. Bundy waited the whole day for news and almost gave up hope, but towards the end of the day, he was told he had visitors, and he went in expecting to see only Jamey there, but in fact Carole Ann and Jamey were there with baby Rosa.

From his prison cell on death row, Ted seemed to be quite happy to play the role of a loving but absent father, writing that he was living "a simple, open, quiet and conscious existence, and am happier, more content, and more full of love than I ever imagined I could be".

Bundy wrote afterwards, "I'm a papa. Lord, I'm in a daze. I still don't believe it. It's like the Christmas of Christmas. It's a lovely dream that's become real. Rosa is so perfectly beautiful. Lord, this is sweet. I've been smiling for over 24 hours straight, or so it seems, ever since I first saw my new daughter yesterday. She was less than 24 hours old when I saw her and the images in my mind of her, then, as I first saw and held her, have been appearing all day and making me blink in disbelief each time I recall her. It's so unreal. There is something to be said for becoming a father in one's thirties. It is so much more special for me now."

Despite the incredible depravity and torture that he visited on innocent young women and the many lives he ruined in the process, he seemed to be able to play a positive role to Rosa, like he had to Liz's daughter Molly a decade earlier. Yet still his cruelty persisted towards the victims of his crimes. With nothing to gain legally from withholding information, he still refused to admit any kind of culpability or share any details about where the grieving families could find the bodies of their relatives. He had a facade to keep up for Carole Ann and his friends who still believed he was innocent.

After Rosa was born, Carole took a secretarial job at the University of Florida and enrolled her son Jamey at Gainesville High School. Jamey had grown up to be a serious young man, very athletic but always reserved, which was only reinforced by the intense media scrutiny that he and his family had been under since Ted was first arrested and imprisoned. At college, Jamey excelled on the football team and wrestling teams. He was never anything but a close ally of Ted's who, like his mother, firmly believed in his stepfather's innocence and wanted nothing more than to see him released and reunited with his mother. Jamey dreamed of them all moving somewhere beautiful, "like Montana", and starting over.

On the legal front, Ted continued to fight the system that had incarcerated him, launching a series of appeals against all three of his death sentences. The first appeal on the verdict from the Chi Omega trial came in 1982. Bundy had enlisted a new lawyer to help him on that case, but it was swiftly rejected by the courts and he was denied even a new hearing. Next, he turned his attention to the Kimberly Leach trial, which he appealed in 1985. But that too was swiftly rejected. Ted's date with Ol' Sparky, the Florida State Prison electric chair, stayed on the books.

In 1986, he hired a young lawyer named Polly Nelson to represent him. She seemed to have more luck than any of the others who had worked for Ted Bundy before. She was the eldest of five children from a town in Minnesota who had begun her career as a social worker before taking up the law at the University of Minnesota. She graduated in 1984 and accepted an offer to the Washington, D.C., law firm of Wilmer, Cutler and Pickering. Two years later, she took on the pro bono assignment of assisting with Bundy's appeals.

Time was running out fast for Bundy. A stay of execution was a huge responsibility for a young lawyer with no criminal experience, but Nelson rose to the challenge and was able to secure a number of stays of execution for Bundy. With the eyes of the general public firmly on her, she acquitted herself well and earned a reputation as someone with substantial legal experience and exposure to complex legal processes, particularly in capital punishment appeals.

In her increasingly desperate bid to save Ted Bundy from the death penalty, she employed a multi-pronged legal strategy that leveraged every available technicality and loophole. At the heart of her approach was the argument that Bundy had been denied effective counsel during his previous trials. She claimed his defence attorneys had failed to adequately represent him, potentially invalidating the convictions and death sentences as a result. She also sought to suppress key evidence, including witness testimonies and forensic analysis, arguing the methods used were flawed and unreliable.

Nelson believed that Bundy was suffering from a mental disorder that had rendered him legally incompetent at the time of his trials, not to mention all of the alcohol and drugs his wife had been slipping him during court recess on trial days.

Recognizing Bundy's increasingly erratic behaviour, Nelson pushed for psychiatric evaluations, aiming to establish that he lacked the mental competency to stand trial in the first place. And she raised concerns about the overwhelming media coverage prejudicing potential jurors, arguing it had undermined Bundy's right to a fair trial. She was convinced that the question of his mental competency was the best, and possibly only, chance at saving his life.

Through 1986, she filed a relentless series of appeals and motions, securing multiple stays of execution as she manoeuvred to keep Bundy alive. It was a strategy of legal gamesmanship, exploiting every procedural avenue in a desperate attempt to cheat the hangman. But in the end, Bundy's crimes were too heinous, his guilt too overwhelming. In the end, she was only delaying the inevitable.

The cost of this pro-bono work was tremendous. The long, drawn-out nature of the appeals and their complexity saw the financial commitment that she had made to Bundy rise until it was worth well over $15 million, a figure that her law firm insisted she would have been able to bill to clients if she wasn't engaged in this charity. In the end, she was dismissed from the firm but was able to turn these experiences into a successful book and gained well-sought-after expertise in the arena of capital punishment.

Following the third and final attempt at a stay of execution, Bundy's date with Ol' Sparky was set for the morning of 24 January 1989. Five days before his execution, when he finally accepted the fact that there would be no more stays of execution, he tried one last gambit. He called Carole up and asked her if he should offer the state a "bones for bodies" deal, which meant that he would receive leniency in return for information on where the missing bodies were buried. Carole was utterly thrown and bewildered by this question. She couldn't get her mind around it. She asked Ted, "But … how are you going to tell them where the bodies are if you had nothing to do with the murders?" He had no good answer to give her.

That was how Carole Ann Boone finally found out that the man she had been defending for over a decade, the man she had loved and believed in for so long, was in fact everything that he had been accused of for so long. She was furious and utterly broken. Ted asked her if he could speak to Rosa and say goodbye to her. Carole managed to say no. She put the phone down and that was the last time they ever spoke.

In truth, she had retreated from the marriage some time earlier in order to focus on raising a child and trying to give Rosa a normal life. They had moved back to Seattle in August of 1986 with Ted's blessings. She had visited him at Thanksgiving in 1987 but there were no visits the following year.

That left only Jamey who was still on Ted's side and still in Florida in the last years of his life. In the days before his execution, Jamey visited Ted in a sanctioned "death-watch, no contact" visit. That was when Ted broke the news to

Jamey that he was planning to cooperate with the police in the hope of a last-minute reprieve. Like his mother, the boy was devastated. Ted told investigator Bob Keppel that seeing "the look in his eyes confirmed my worst fears. He was just absolutely astounded. He couldn't understand. He was writing me questions, just furiously writing questions. I could see how really bewildered he was. And I need to give him and others a chance to know what was really going on. What it was really like, from me ..."

When it came time for the press conference where Bundy was planning to share what he knew, Jamey began literally begging him not to do it. He could just imagine the effect it would have on his mother to hear all the details of what he had done. He honestly would prefer that Ted just took his secrets to the grave with him. He told him "you've hurt Mom enough", and Bundy must have agreed with that summation because he cancelled the press conference.

His legal team were also convinced that confessing would not do him any good at this stage, but Bundy must have felt like he needed to do something to try and save his skin, so he met with a group of detectives and shared what he remembered and tried to give some insight into the criminal mind of a serial killer.

Still, no reprieve was forthcoming. In the final days before the execution, Jamey managed to find the strength to go and visit his stepfather once more, even though he was still reeling from the revelations from a few days earlier that had shaken the foundations of his world. Standing before his stepfather, Jamey was granted permission to hug the convicted man and share a few personal moments with him. Ted was also granted a last phone call, and he listed Carole Ann Boone as the person he would like to call. But prison records reveal that, for some reason or other, he changed his mind and hung up, deciding not to complete the call before Carole had to decide whether or not she would pick up.

The night before his execution, he participated in an interview with the religious broadcaster, James Dobson, and attempted to blame everything that he had done on the twin addictions of alcohol and pornography. After it was over, Dobson told a press conference, "There was a great deal of remorse. He wept several times while talking to me." In the on-camera interview, a gaunt and teary-eyed Bundy explained how he had met a lot of men just like him in prison and "without exception, every single one of them was deeply influenced and consumed by an addiction to pornography".

Crowds began to gather outside the prison on the day before his execution, and they only got larger and larger as the night progressed. Many were young college students who used it as a macabre occasion to get drunk and celebrate the state's vengeance on the man who had stalked their campuses. Television crews arrived with large satellite trucks and set up their equipment, ready to share the news of the notorious killer's final demise with the world. The anger and seething hatred in the crowd were on full display all through the night. A cottage industry of Bundy memorabilia sprung up out of nowhere. Homemade signs implored Ted to "Burn in Hell" and instructed the prison guards to crank up Ol' Sparky. Bundy heard the crowds cheering and setting off fireworks in the distance around the prison and was bemused by it. "They're crazy," he said. "They think I'm crazy but they're crazy."

On the morning of the execution, he was given a final meal consisting of steak, eggs, hash browns and toast, but he declined to eat anything. Then the prison guards shaved Bundy's head and his right calf in order to improve contact with the copper electrodes that would soon be attached to his body, before leading him into the death chamber shortly before 7am.

"He was white as a sheet," remembers Bob Dekle, the lawyer who had prosecuted Bundy and was one of a few witnesses allowed into the viewing section behind the glass wall facing the electric chair.

When he was seated, Bundy was asked if he had any final words to say, and he muttered a few words about being sorry that he had caused so much trouble. Then he was strapped into the chair and a leather skull cap with a black hood was lowered onto his head.

The machine was turned on, and in that moment, the life of one of the most heinous serial killers of modern times was erased from the world.

20

What to Make of Ted Bundy
and His Twisted Mind

There are few images that could be more macabre than this: a group of scientists poring over the extracted brain of a man who has been put to death in the electric chair for brutally murdering dozens of young women.

And yet, something about it makes sense. Even in the world of murder, Ted Bundy was an outlier, a bizarre curio of sorts. Even in the rare situation of serial killing, he stands out as one of the most brutal and busy killers whose public persona and genuine personality could not have been more at odds.

And it is a sad indictment on us all that a man of such depravity, who robbed so many young women of their lives and futures, should receive such attention even decades after his death. He caused immeasurable pain for a great many people, snuffed out all potential and opportunity for a great many others, conducted himself with no sense of remorse and, ultimately, stood out as an extreme example of how defective a human being can be.

In an ideal world, society would not give him any more of the attention he craved, but the extreme facts of his case have made the public want to understand such a dark mind and, at the very least, try to fathom what he was thinking when he did what he did.

Long before his brain was taken from his lifeless body into a laboratory for closer scrutiny, his mind had become a site of intrigue to psychologists and psychiatrists, journalists and the public, true crime aficionados, and anyone with an interest in the human mind and how deviant it can be. Tragically, his mind also revealed itself to be a source of complete mystery, even to those who genuinely loved him and believed in his innocence until the indisputable truths emerged.

Bundy's confessions about his crimes, made shortly before his execution in 1989 when he was 42 years old, are a complex mix of confirmed admissions and questionable claims. He claimed to have murdered thirty women across several states, but there are experts who firmly believe the actual number could be significantly higher, perhaps even as many as one hundred. There's a good chance that he had killed a lot earlier than the public ever discovered, and that a few victims fell through the gaps and were never discovered. No one will ever know.

Throughout his life, Bundy lied, embellished stories, played "injured" to lure victims, used the gaps in the criminal justice system to his favour. And when the time came to bring some closure, at the very least, to the families he had shattered, he continued to obfuscate until the very end.

Some of the narratives he shared on death row were corroborated by evidence and investigation, but others were riddled with discrepancies. He went about using confessions as a means to gain sympathy, delay his execution or elicit leniency from those deciding on his punishment.

But ultimately, this last bout of deception and lies came to nothing: he was electrocuted to death, taking his secrets with him to the grave.

THERE WERE TWO TEDS

One of the first people to analyze the mind of Bundy was a psychologist at the Utah State Prison named Dr Al Carlisle. He was initially saddled with evaluating Ted Bundy in 1976 for a pre-sentencing report regarding the Carol DaRonch kidnapping case.

Evaluating Bundy's psychological profile and risk level were part of a pre-sentencing assessment for probation and parole considerations. His mental state, personality traits and potential threat to society would come under the spotlight at that time, but his psychological insights would become highly influential three years later when the murder trial was underway.

"There was a side to Ted that he didn't want other people to see," noted Carlisle. "It was almost like there were two Teds. There was the public Ted that people saw, the charming, intellectual person. But there was this other Ted, this predator, this person who got a thrill out of hurting people."

His evaluation in 1976 included not only standard psychological tests but also extensive interviews with people from his past.

Until mandated by the court to undergo this evaluation, Bundy had neither sought nor received any form of psychological intervention, and it was now up to Carlisle to begin that first investigation. In an ideal world, such assessments would help professionals understand the mindset of a criminal and also predict the risk factor of them repeating their crimes if given the opportunity.

But in the case of a manipulative serial killer like Bundy, any genuine assessment was hindered by his extreme secretiveness and the facade he expertly created of being normal and even charming. Carlisle noted that Bundy could be pleasant and affable, even while harbouring intense rage and a compulsive desire to kill. Carlisle was among the first to grasp the intensity of Bundy's suppressed rage, realizing that it was this emotion that likely fuelled all of his violent acts.

He wrote, "It became apparent to me that Ted had a lot of anger. He had resentment. He was building up pressure that he needed to release, and that release came through violence."

Because Bundy had studied psychology and was not happy about being evaluated, he often answered the questions in ways that he thought would suit him rather than to give a sense of his authentic personality.

However, because Carlisle was able to sometimes see through the facade, and because he had conducted thorough research, gathering insights from numerous individuals who were acquainted with Bundy over the course of his life, he was able to take a wider view.

He discovered more about Bundy's darker side, that he was a habitual liar, broke rules without conscience, stole items on a whim and frequently changed his persona to suit different situations. One only needs to recall his charade as an injured man with an arm in a bandage at Lake Sammamish.

"Ted could be whatever he thought people wanted him to be. He could manipulate and he could con. He could make you feel like you were the only person in the room, and he could charm the socks off of you," Carlisle noted.

He consistently found Bundy to be approachable yet highly evasive during discussions, always pulling the conversation away in another direction. Other warning signs emerged: there were contradictions, gaps in his retelling of stories and the timeframes associated with them, and a general lack of authenticity.

He suggested that various factors contributed to Bundy's violent personality, including influences and experiences from his formative years that shaped the "crazy necrophile" image associated with him.

In recorded conversations, Bundy attributed his early exposure to pornography as a contributing factor. However, Carlisle viewed this explanation as overly simplistic. He elaborated on how Bundy transitioned from sexual fantasies to murder and necrophilia.

DREAMING UP HIS OWN SCENARIOS

Carlisle is among the few mental health professionals who spent time with Bundy in various contexts, and he suggests that the capacity for repeated killings while appearing normal (such as aspiring to be governor) developed through three main processes.

The first was "fantasy". In this process, Bundy would have imagined a scenario for entertainment or comfort. The second, "dissociation", would have seen Bundy avoiding any uncomfortable emotions or memories. And the third, "compartmentalization", would see him assigning different thoughts and images to specific mental categories in an effort to maintain boundaries between them.

In short, Bundy could dream up a scenario that fitted his fantasy (raping and murdering a student in her bed), then cut himself off from any emotions about making it real (paying no mind at all to the student as a human being with a life and feelings), and then act like a "normal" person the next day, going about his business without reflecting on the horrors of the night before, as if it never happened.

Through these processes, Carlisle noted, serial killers like Bundy are able to maintain a public image that appears "good" while simultaneously harbouring a dark side that indulges their murderous fantasies. Many of these individuals have experienced painful memories from abuse, disappointment, humiliation, frustration or bullying and, as a result, turn to fantasies for comfort. They may even create alternate identities that offer them a sense of power or status. Bundy, for instance, developed elaborate hero fantasies that eventually morphed into desires for sexual possession.

According to Carlisle, Bundy's fantasies might have served as a means to express unacceptable impulses, desires and aspirations. As everyday life becomes dull or disappointing, the allure of fantasy only intensifies.

Over time, the violent aspects of these fantasies may have become more pronounced through mental rehearsal or opportunity, leading to an addiction to these unrestricted thoughts. Carlisle believed this is how Bundy would have described his experience.

Ultimately, killers like Bundy learn to conceal their secrets from others by developing different value systems for various aspects of their lives. This allows them to function normally in one realm while simultaneously seeking out victims and engaging in deviant behaviour in another.

Carlisle hypothesized that compartmentalization is a process everyone can engage in to some extent; it exists on a spectrum ranging from healthy forms – like an actor immersing themselves in a role – to the destructive compartmentalization seen in individuals like Bundy, which can lead to violence.

As fantasy increasingly merges with reality, Carlisle stated that it likely became difficult – if not impossible – for good and evil to coexist within the same mind. To cope with this internal conflict, Bundy had to find ways to lessen the divide between his two personas. His understanding of right and wrong evolved over time; behaviours he deemed wrong as a child became acceptable in his early teens and eventually desirable by late adolescence.

Among the tools used by Carlisle in his assessment was the Thematic Apperception Test, where the subject looks at an image and describes what they see, adding layers of perception as they go. Bundy had clear ideas about gender roles for women. Reportedly, during his childhood, his grandmother (whom he believed to be his mother) was submissive, while his grandfather (whom he thought was his father) was dominant and abusive.

Despite this abusive behaviour from his grandfather, his grandmother continued to cater to him, never standing up for herself. This dynamic likely shaped Bundy's perception of gender roles, reflecting the influence of his early family life before his mother took him away. She recognized the negative impact her father had on him and later married Johnny Bundy, who was said to be a good father. However, it seems it was too late for Bundy, as he had already formed a fixed image of gender roles and never gave Johnny Bundy a chance.

The thematic apperception image serves as an example of these dynamics.

Carlisle suggested that Bundy's use of the terms "sinister" and "gentleman" when looking at the images in the test was intriguing because it highlighted two conflicting personality traits: Bundy was a murderer who worked hard to present himself as a rising politician and an emotionally controlled intellectual.

THE DARK TRIAD

Bundy is often analyzed through the lens of the Dark Triad personality traits, which consist of the three traits of psychopathy, narcissism and Machiavellianism. These traits help to explain his manipulative behaviour, lack of empathy, and desire to carry out his violent fantasies.

Psychopathy is characterized by a profound lack of empathy, shallow emotions and manipulative behaviour. With hindsight, when professionals were able to build a composite picture of the vicious crimes he committed and how he went about luring his victims, it was clear that he exhibited several psychopathic traits.

He could understand others' emotions cognitively but did not feel them, allowing him to manipulate victims effectively without remorse. For example, when he lured the victims at Lake Sammamish, he had deliberately constructed a scenario in which they'd feel sympathy for him because his arm was in a sling, and he could then abuse their goodwill. Superficial charm was learned and wielded as a weapon alongside this.

Just as calculated was his methodical approach to abduction and murder. He would strategize and plan his predatory actions, which is typical of psychopathic behaviour.

Many psychopaths can present themselves as charming and normal, effectively masking their violent tendencies. They may employ a "mask of sanity", allowing them to blend into society while concealing their true nature.

Then there was the narcissism. Bundy's grandiose sense of self-importance was just as pronounced as his ability to fake humility. He viewed himself as being special and above the law, and most importantly in terms of narcissistic traits, he engaged in exploitative relationships. In other words, he used people as tools for his own gratification.

Finally, Bundy was the epitome of Machiavellianism. His personality was characterized by manipulation, cunning, deceit and focus on self-interest at the expense of others. He was indifferent to morality when it came to satisfying his thirst for murder, and he was very calculated in how he went about his crimes and his attempts to evade punishment.

HOW COMMON IS A KILLER LIKE BUNDY?

With the extraordinary amount of gun violence in the United States, lay members of the public sometimes conflate the various types of mass murderers who cause the deaths of many people. But there are distinctive differences, and Bundy is a classic example of only one of those.

Mass murderers are the ones who kill three or more people in one go and usually at a single location. Think of your typical school shooter who bursts into a classroom and mows down innocent learners.

Spree killers, on the other hand, typically kill two or more people over a very short space of time but usually at multiple locations. There is no "cooling off" period between the killings.

Then you get your serial killers, and this is where Ted Bundy comes in, although he did also engage in limited spree killing on the night of the Chi Omega attacks.

A serial killer is defined as an individual who commits three or more murders over a significant period of time, with distinct cooling-off periods between the murders. The killings are typically motivated by psychological gratification, and victims often share common characteristics.

As illustrated in this book, Bundy was the living definition of a serial killer. There were typically cooling-off periods lasting up to a few weeks between his murders, and almost every time, the victims were petite and had long brown hair parted in the middle.

But most striking of all is this: the vast majority of serial killers are male, with a significant proportion being white. They are often aged between 25 and 34 years old at the time of their first known murder.

So how common is a serial killer like Bundy?

The world population is currently around eight billion. If we consider a rough estimate of 2,100 unidentified serial killers, as suggested by some experts, this would represent about 0.00002625 per cent of the global population.

That is an extremely low rate, and for that, we should be truly grateful.

IN HIS OWN WORDS

Bundy imagined a world where many other men were just like him. He once said, "We serial killers are your sons, we are your husbands, we are everywhere. And there will be more of your children dead tomorrow."

Strangely, however, he resented any perception that he was defective, saying, "I'm not an animal, and I'm not crazy and I'm not a split personality. That's all there is to it. People refuse to believe that. That's their problem."

But the most chilling of all are his descriptions of his own actions and what drove them.

He once said, "Murder is not just a crime of lust or violence. It becomes possession. They are part of you ... [the victim] becomes a part of you, and you [two] are forever one."

Perhaps the single most telling utterance that lifts at least a small part of the veil off his mind for normal people to imagine its dark machinations is this: "When you feel the last bit of breath leaving their body, you're looking into their eyes. A person in that situation is God!"

Bibliography

Bartosch, Jamie. 12 June 2020. Biography.com. *Meet Elizabeth Kloepfer, Ted Bundy's former girlfriend.* https://www.biography.com/crime/ted-bundy-elizabeth-kloepfer

Bruney, Gabrielle. 6 May 2019. Esquire.com. *Ted Bundy acting as his own lawyer made for a sadistic show* during his *murder trials.* https://www.esquire.com/entertainment/a27375563/ted-bundy-trial-lawyer-true-story/

Capital Punishment in Context. *Media influence in capital cases.* https://capitalpunishmentincontext.org/issues/media

Carlson, Adam. 18 December 2022. People magazine. *'Girl who got away': The true story of Ted Bundy survivor Carol DaRonch and her life now.* https://people.com/crime/true-story-carol-daronch-now-ted-bundy-movie/

DeLisi, Matt. *Ted Bundy and The Unsolved Murder Epidemic* (Palgrave Macmillan, 2023)

Florida State University Law Library. Supreme Court of Florida, No. 59128. https://library.law.fsu.edu/Digital-Collections/flsupct/dockets/59128/op-59128.pdf

Fraga, Kaleena. 1 October 2023. AllThatsInteresting.com. *How many people did Ted Bundy kill? The stories of his victims.* https://allthatsinteresting.com/ted-bundy-victims

Jean, Tiffany. 2019. Killer in the Archives blog. *A profile of Carole Ann Boone.* https://killerinthearchives.blog/a-profile-of-carole-ann-boone/

Jurewicz-Woods, Jessica. April 2022. Another Bundy Blog. https://anotherbundyblog.com/

Justia. 21 June 1984. Supreme Court of Florida, No. 57772. https://law.justia.com/cases/florida/supreme-court/1984/57772-0.html

Kelley, Ash & Urquhart, Alaina. 29 May 2018. Morbid: A True Crime Podcast. *Ted Bundy.* https://open.spotify.com/episode/2sKe749IhzGDIgrwSS1iRB

Keppel, Robert D. and Birnes, William J. *The Riverman: Ted Bundy and I Hunt for the Green River Killer* (Pocket Books, 2010)

Kranc, Lauren. 18 November 2020. Esquire.com. *Dr. Dorothy Otnow Lewis knew a different Ted Bundy.* https://www.esquire.com/entertainment/movies/a34703418/dr-dorothy-otnow-lewis-crazy-not-insane-interview-today/

Macpherson, Myra. May 1989. *Vanity Fair.* "The roots of evil". https://archive.vanityfair.com/article/1989/5/the-roots-of-evil

Merryweather, Cheish. 16 February 2020. Top 9 newly found photos of Ted Bundy. https://listverse.com/2020/02/16/top-9-newly-found-photos-of-ted-bundy-and-their-chilling-backstories/

Michaud, Stephen G. & Aynesworth, Hugh. *Ted Bundy: Conversations with a Killer* (Harper Audio, 2019)

Nixon, Christina. 27 March 2023. Iconic Magazine Online. *Ted Bundy and the history of the Elizabeth Lund Home.* https://iconicmagazineonline.com/2019/12/13/ted-bundy-and-the-history-of-the-elizabeth-lund-home/

Nordheimer, Jon. 10 December 1978. The New York Times. *All-American boy on trial.* https://www.nytimes.com/1978/12/10/archives/allamerican-boy-on-trial-ted-bundy.html

Norton, Allie. 13 February 2018. Weartv.com. *Bundy's last stop: Recounting a serial killer's arrest 40 years later.* https://weartv.com/news/local/bundys-last-stop-recounting-a-serial-killers-arrest-40-years-later

Oldham, Scott. 5 May 2019. CarandDriver.com. *How Ted Bundy made humble Volkswagen Bugs into implements of evil.* https://www.caranddriver.com/features/a27357775/ted-bundys-volkswagens/

Picotti, Tyler. 26 June 2024. Biography.com. *Ted Bundy.* https://www.biography.com/crime/ted-bundy

Rule, Ann. *The Stranger Beside Me* (Simon & Schuster Audio, 2012)

Sederstrom, Jill. 20 August 2019. Oxygen.com. *What was Ted Bundy's childhood like?* https://www.oxygen.com/martinis-murder/what-was-ted-bundys-childhood-like

Sederstrom, Jill. 4 October 2020. Oxygen.com. *Ted Bundy's first known victim believes a random coincidence saved her life.* https://www.oxygen.com/true-crime-buzz/what-does-ted-bundy-victim-karen-sparks-believe-kept-her-alive

Sederstrom, Jill. 31 January 2019. Oxygen.com. *Who was Lynda Ann Healy?* https://www.oxygen.com/martinis-murder/who-was-lynda-ann-healy-ted-bundy-first-known-victim

Sederstrom, Jill. 31 January 2020. Oxygen.com. *Who Was Ted Bundy's Wife, Carole Ann Boone?* https://www.oxygen.com/martinis-murder/who-was-ted-bundys-wife-carole-ann-boone

Taudte, Jeca, Gowen, Gwen & Francis, Enjolie. 16 February 2019. ABC News. *Remembering Kimberly Leach.* https://abcnews.go.com/US/remembering-kimberly-leach-12-ted-bundys-victim-world/story?id=60912704

Tron, Gina. 24 January 2019. Oxygen.com. *Who was Diane Edwards?* https://www.oxygen.com/martinis-murder/who-was-diane-edwards-ted-bundys-first-girlfriend

Unicef. 2017. *Violence in early childhood.* https://www.unicef.org/
lac/media/691/file/PDF%20Violence%20in%20early%20
childhood.pdf

Wilkinson, Amy. 4 May 2019. *Ted Bundy worked at a suicide
hotline—Here's why, according to a forensic psychologist.* https://
www.womenshealthmag.com/health/a27354040/ted-
bundy-movie-suicide-hotline-forensic-psychologist/